JAMES MADISON, AMERICAN PROPHET

by Duane L. Ostler

ISBN-13: 978-1514876671
ISBN-10: 1514876671

Cover art: "James Madison,"
by John Vanderlyn, 1816.

Interior art: Ch. 1 "James Madison,"
by John Vanderlyn, 1816; Ch. 2 "James Madison," by Gilbert
Stuart, 1828; Ch. 3 Original Bill of Rights; Ch. 4 "Our
Overworked Supreme Court," by Joseph F. Keppler in Puck
magazine, 1885; Ch. 5 "Battle of Lake Erie," by William H.
Powell, 1873; Ch. 6 $5,000 bill with James Madison; Ch. 7
Recreated colonial dance scene, photograph by Underwood &
Underwood, 1900; Ch. 8 "This is what the 'Freedom of
Worship' bill means - can we hold evil in check?" by Joseph
F. Keppler in Puck magazine, 1885; Ch. 9 "A Slave Auction
at the South," sketch by Theodore R. Davis, 1861; Ch. 10
"James Madison," by Thomas Sully, between 1809-1817.

TABLE OF CONTENTS

This book is dedicated to the memory of
Professor Robert E. Riggs,
Constitutional scholar,
and the one who started me on my path.

CHAPTER ONE
Introduction

James Madison saw our day. While he had no medium or time machine that allowed him to do it, he nonetheless saw more than 200 years into the future, viewing our conditions and situation, politically and culturally. He saw our turmoil, our political uncertainty and occasional financial chaos, our flirtations with war and uneasy peace, our political party-bashing and Supreme Court activism. And as America's pre-eminent political visionary, he also saw how these problems could be solved.

But of course, many today don't believe such a thing. How could that short little man, dead now for over 175 years have any idea of what we face today? Could he have contemplated Ebay sales on the internet, the atomic bomb or modern terrorism? Did he really foresee traffic jams, computer viruses, microwavable noodles or mind-numbing TV commercials? Did he have any idea that satellites would circle the globe, that cell phones might drop calls while driving a car 75 miles per hour through a canyon, or that the TSA would perform pat down searches of travelers at airports? How on earth could he have known all that?

Well, of course he didn't know such fine details of modern society. Even his wildest nightmares couldn't have produced such ideas. And because of this truth, in our modern arrogance we tend to think that somehow means he also lacked any real understanding of our political and cultural challenges today--as if modern technology and the inventions of the last 200 years somehow have changed everything in life so much that there are no common principles or concepts between his time and ours. Viewed this way, his era is separated from ours by a great divide, as if either his generation or ours were an alien race originating from another planet.

But if he really is lost in a fallen and long-dead era from another world, how can anyone explain such wonderfully modern, prophetic and pithy statements of his as these?

"The law does bear fruit, but it is sour fruit."

"A bad cause seldom fails to betray itself."

"All men having power ought to be distrusted to a certain degree."

"The circulation of confidence is better than the circulation of money."

Seriously, if a man on the street were to hear these statements today, he would think they came from a political talk show host on the radio this morning, not from the mind of the fourth president of the United States and 'Father of the Constitution,' now long since deceased - a man who saw our day.

The simple reality is, Madison was a genius. His perception of government and how it worked far exceeds that of almost everyone today. In the pages that follow we will see his genius demonstrated again and again, as we address modern difficulties with Supreme Court activism, terrorists and war, banking and economic woes, and a host of other problems. It is incredible that this short little man who lived

200 years ago could have such an amazing perception of our problems, even after all these years. But then again, perhaps the reason is that most of our modern conundrums (such as abortion, terrorism, the right to die, banking fiascos, drug trafficking, etc., etc.) are not based on technology but on morality and common sense. And those are things he understood exceptionally well.

Many scholars have tried to criticize Madison over the years, to bring him down to their level of thinking, to make him seem like a normal guy who just got lucky by being in the right place at the right time. Such efforts fall flat when a simple resort to Madison's own words is made. If we stop reading things written about Madison by scholars, and instead start reading what he wrote, then we will see him in an entirely different light. Then we will begin to see his genius, his vision, his incredibly accurate perceptions of political reality, and--most important of all--his counsel on how to extricate ourselves from the messes we have made for ourselves in this modern era. For he truly saw our day.

Of course, this acknowledgment condemns the very volume you are holding in your hands, since it too falls short of Madison's brilliant mental powers. What is presented here was once again filtered through a modern scholar--me--and is given to readers piecemeal, spewing the bits and pieces that I, with my weaker mind, have presumed are the most important. I have no doubt that if Madison had compiled this volume, it would be vastly different. But sadly for us, he is not here and cannot do the job himself. And so I make my meager effort, saved if anything by the presence of Madison's words themselves on these pages-- words which I quote at every opportunity.

Indeed, that is my greatest hope in respect to this volume - that the things presented here will spark the reader with a desire to go to the source, to read Madison himself. That is where the real jewels of wisdom from this American prophet are to be found. Only in that way can we avoid the stretched and biased views of modern scholars, with all their peculiar notions of what is most important to present about him. And only in that way can we completely discover for ourselves the solutions that he foresaw to the horrible problems we face in our troubled world today.

CHAPTER TWO
This Was No 'Withered Little Apple John'

Before beginning our journey of discovery into the prophetic insights of Madison in our day, it is helpful to gain some appreciation for just who he was, and what role he played in history. This chapter will provide a brief chronology of the life and times of Madison, and will hopefully make clear why he was chosen to be the subject of this volume rather than the other spectacular luminaries of his day such as Thomas Jefferson, George Washington, Benjamin Franklin or John Adams. While author Washington Irving described Madison as a 'withered little apple-john,' we will soon see that such a description is the exact opposite of the truth.

Madison was born on March 16, 1751 at King George County, Virginia. Young James was the oldest of twelve children and took the name of his father, thereby becoming James Madison, Jr. At age eleven he began attending a school seventy miles from his home run by Scotsman Donald Robertson. Madison studied under Robertson for five years, far surpassing the school youth of today by learning Latin and Greek, as well as a smattering of French and Spanish (all with a Scottish brogue, of course, due to his teacher), in addition to mathematics and history. After this, he returned home where he was tutored by the Reverend Thomas Martin, a recent graduate of Princeton in New Jersey. Martin ultimately convinced Madison's family that the boy should attend college at Princeton under its new president John Witherspoon, rather than going to William and Mary College in nearby Williamsburg. When Madison departed for Princeton at the age of eighteen to start college, he was already "better educated than many a present-day holder of a baccalaureate degree."[1]

At Princeton, Madison applied himself so diligently and single-mindedly to his work that he completed his four year degree in two years. He then stayed on for an additional six months to study Hebrew and law. Madison apparently thought that he might become a practicing attorney. However, he soon made the discovery that law was not particularly satisfying. He later referred to the study of law as "coarse and dry," and further said that leaving worthwhile pursuits to study law "is like leaving a pleasant and flourishing field for a barren desert; perhaps I should not say barren either, because the law does bear fruit, but it is sour fruit."[2]

All too soon, Madison's education at Princeton and tutelage under John Witherspoon was over. Benjamin Rush, signer of the Declaration of Independence, said of Madison's time at Princeton that "[h]is only relaxation from study consisted in walking and conversation. Such was the character he acquired while at college, that Dr. Witherspoon said of him to Mr. Jefferson (from whom I received the anecdote) that during the whole time he was under his tuition he never knew him to do nor to say an improper thing."[3]

In 1772 Madison returned to his home in Virginia exhausted from over study. He was a small and weak man, not having been endowed with a large impressive frame like the six foot three George Washington, or the six foot two Thomas Jefferson. Madison stood only five feet six inches tall, and weighed roughly 100 pounds. He had delicate health, and conjectured after returning from Princeton that he was "not to expect a long or healthy life." Because of this he stated that he had little ambition to acquire worldly goods, since it seemed pointless to "set about anything that is difficult in acquiring and useless in possessing after one has exchanged time for eternity."[4] This was clearly a rare instance where his prophetic insights completely failed him, since he ended up living to the ripe old age of 85.

But his astute perceptions of reality did not fail him in other respects. In 1773 he expressed the following observation regarding those who profess friendship, but who are in reality insincere: "When I observe anyone over complaisant to me in his professions and promises, I am tempted to interpret his language thus: 'As I have no real esteem for you, and for certain reasons think it expedient to appear well in your eye, I endeavor to varnish falsehood with politeness, which I think I can do in so ingenious a manner that so vain a blockhead as you cannot see through it.'"[5] Once again, this is not the sort of thing we expect our stodgy image of Madison to say.

It was the revolution that launched Madison into his long and brilliant political career. While most young men went off to fight, given his frail health he went into politics instead. In December, 1774, he was elected to the Orange County Committee of Safety, and in early 1776 he was elected as a delegate from his county to attend a convention in Williamsburg that drafted the first constitution and declaration of rights for Virginia. Hence, from the very beginning Madison was involved in the creation of constitutions and bills of rights. He suggested a change of wording to broaden religious freedom in the Virginia Declaration of Rights, thereby setting one of the primary themes of his life as discussed more fully in chapter 8. His suggestion was adopted.

After losing his bid for reelection due in part to his refusal to give whiskey to bribe voters, the Virginia Assembly itself appointed him to the governor's cabinet, known as the 'Council of Safety.' He worked closely with Governors Patrick Henry and later Thomas Jefferson, with whom he formed a particularly close friendship. Then in 1779, Madison was elected as a delegate from Virginia to the Continental Congress in Philadelphia, where he served for three years. One of Madison's chief contributions while in the Continental Congress dealt with the national debt. Financial conditions at the time were horrific and chaotic. The soldiers of General Washington's army often went unpaid, and national debts languished for years. States were unwilling to tax their citizens to fill the pressing financial needs since the war was being fought over taxes, and the states knew their citizens wouldn't stand for it. After all, how could they convince their citizens to pay higher taxes to fight a war to reduce taxes?

In the midst of this chaos, Madison joined with others in proposing a tax solely on imports. This flow of income would be combined with individual allocations of the states to pay off the debt. It was a compromise from the more rigorous national taxing authority Madison really wanted, but which he knew could not be obtained from the wrangling states. This plan was ultimately adopted. While in Congress, Madison also was involved in Virginia's giving up of much of its western lands to the union.

At the close of the Revolutionary War in 1783, after three years in Congress, Madison was forced to leave. The Articles of Confederation prevented a representative from serving more than 3 years out of every 6. Madison returned to the Virginia legislature where he battled Patrick Henry and other entrenched politicians over religious freedom and adoption of a new and revised code of laws. Patrick Henry's scheme to use general tax funds to pay the clergy evoked one of Madison's most passionate and well reasoned political essays--a "Memorial and Remonstrance Against Religious Assessments," which is further discussed in chapter 8.

While Madison was enjoying some success in state politics during his three years in the Virginia Assembly, his fears for the union robbed any sense of satisfaction such victories gave him. With Shays Rebellion in Massachusetts and constant bickering among the states, Madison feared more and more that the American experiment in freedom would result in several independent leagues of states, each bent on their own goals. He was not alone in this view. Many other patriots of the era were equally alarmed at the chaos that was fast engulfing America. When a convention was called for state representatives to deal with trade and commerce in 1786 in Annapolis, Madison gladly served as one of the delegates from Virginia. Unfortunately, only five states were represented when the convention convened, effectively terminating its effectiveness.

But the Annapolis Convention did achieve one notable goal--its delegates called for a new convention of all the states in Philadelphia the following May. Madison had no desire to see this effort fail, so he courted the attendance of the one man in America whose presence might guarantee the convention's success--his distant relative (first cousin twice removed) George Washington. At first resistant, Washington ultimately agreed to attend. The resultant convention was a roaring success, as it created a new constitutional form of government. Madison was its chief architect, framing the 'Virginia Plan' that was presented at the outset of the convention and which served as the basis for debate and the structural guide for the final constitution. As will be more fully explained in later chapters, Madison's proposals for creation of government at the convention were far-sighted and visionary to say the least, and many of them have since been adopted in one fashion or another even though they may have been refused in his day. As is discussed more fully in chapter 3, chief among his goals was a 'legislative veto,' by which the federal congress could overturn any and all state laws. By this method, Madison hoped the more diverse federal government could overcome abuses of rights that sometimes occurred in the state legislatures. He was bitterly disappointed when this proposal was turned down by the convention.

Although not fully satisfied with the final constitution, Madison nonetheless threw his considerable talents behind its ratification by the states. He knew the document still had much good in it, and that nothing better was going to come along. He was particularly instrumental in the ratification process in Virginia, knowing as he did that no federal union could succeed without the approval of his home state. In the intense debates, he countered Patrick Henry's passionate speeches with clear, articulate and well-reasoned expressions of logic. At the time of Virginia's ratification the requisite number of state approvals was met, and the Constitution commenced operation.

In the first federal elections, Madison ran against his good friend James Monroe for a seat in the House of Representatives. He won, and was among the first to arrive at the nation's capital (at that time) in Philadelphia, in March 1789. To his chagrin, a quorum of both houses sufficient to get the new government started by officially counting the electoral votes for president did not occur until a month later, on April 6, 1789. Of course, everyone knew that George Washington had been elected president even before the votes were counted.

One of Madison's first acts in the House was to propose a series of amendments to the constitution, consisting of a bill of rights. He did so over the objections of most of his colleagues, who were convinced that more pressing issues should be dealt with, such as the horrendous political and economic chaos that reined at that time. But with typical prophetic insight, Madison persisted, and the amendments were ultimately debated and adopted. As discussed in chapter 3, it is a curious irony that Madison did not present the amendments because he felt a need for a bill of rights. Indeed, he believed bills of rights were either dangerous or unnecessary! However, he made the proposal and pushed the amendments through a reluctant congress in order to outmaneuver opponents of the constitution who were calling for a second constitutional convention. Madison knew that if his amendments were quickly adopted, calls for a second convention would almost certainly die away and the structure of the constitution would not be altered. Naturally, he made sure none of his proposed amendments threatened the structure of the Constitution, and that they only dealt with straightforward 'rights' issues that were largely above debate. His colleagues agreed that the new amendments were innocuous. As stated by Samuel Livermore, representative from New Hampshire, Madison's bill of rights were no "more than a pinch of snuff; they went to secure rights never in danger."[6]

In the first congress, Madison also introduced a revenue bill setting duties on foreign imports, and moved for the establishment of executive departments such as foreign affairs, war and treasury. For the next several years, Madison remained as one of the most influential members of Congress, rising often in the debates in the House. He was particularly outspoken on issues of constitutional interpretation, such as Hamilton's proposal for a national bank. As is discussed in chapter 6, Madison opposed the bank, partly because he felt there was no constitutional support for such an institution, and that the "necessary and proper clause" was not sufficient authority to create it. Notwithstanding his opposition, the bank bill was passed and signed into law by President Washington. During Madison's own presidency years later, he switched positions and supported the bank as a necessary institution, on the basis that it had now become an established and traditional entity of government.

One of the most striking elements to emerge during this era were political parties. As Washington's presidency passed into its second term, the partisan wars between the Hamiltonian 'Federalists' and the 'Republican' followers of Jefferson and Madison increased. The fact that both Hamilton and Jefferson were part of Washington's cabinet added to the tension. Seeing Washington turn more and more to Hamilton and his policies, Jefferson ultimately resigned his post as Secretary of State in disgust and retreated to Virginia. This left Madison alone to lead the new Republican opposition party in the political battles that raged in the nation's capital.

But as the dispute over the location of the new national capital demonstrates, the political battles engaged in by the warring parties were not always as bitter as they seemed. In 1790, before Jefferson's resignation, he, Hamilton and Madison did something that most political rivals rarely do--they had dinner together. However, this particular dinner was more than a mere culinary enjoyment. During the course of the meal a compromise was reached on some of the most pressing political issues of the day. Madison and Jefferson agreed to cease their opposition to Hamilton's plan that the national government should assume the state's war debts, in exchange for the nation's capital being located in the south on the banks of the Potomac. These three were bitter rivals and often at odds over how the government was to be administered, and yet were nonetheless united in their devotion to the union.

Relations between Jefferson and Madison and John Adams were bitter as well. After Adams narrowly defeated Jefferson for the presidency in the 1796 election, he went on to become the most hated subject of attack by the Republicans. Enactment by a Federalist dominated congress of the 'Alien and Sedition Acts' of 1798 intensified the battle. These acts allowed Adams to deport anyone he thought was a danger to liberty, and allowed the Federalist-dominated federal courts to criminally prosecute critics of the government. Republicans rightly asserted that this law was a blatant violation of the First Amendment. Hence, even at this early stage we see vindication of one of Madison's prophetic fears about a bill of rights--that the mere existence of such a document did not guarantee that rights would actually be protected from a faction in the legislature. Incensed at these acts, Madison and Jefferson penned the 'Virginia and Kentucky Resolutions,' which soundly criticized these federal laws.

And then relief came. The Federalist ship of state crashed on the rocks, and in the election of 1800 Thomas Jefferson gained the presidency. Madison became his Secretary of State, a position which he faithfully filled for eight years. His stature in national politics was now secure, and he was clearly known as President Jefferson's right-hand man. He was heavily involved in the Louisiana Purchase of 1803 from Napoleon, and was one of the named parties in the famous case of 'Marbury v. Madison,' in which the Supreme Court established its right to overturn laws of congress as being unconstitutional.

But the most pressing issue as Jefferson's presidency proceeded was the increasingly impossible condition of shipping and trade.

Britain and France were now at war with each other, and these two major world powers treated the weak and fledgling U.S. like a piece of driftwood in a raging sea storm. Each nation enacted absurd shipping laws, making it 'criminal' for another nation (particularly the U.S.) to trade with the other without their approval. On the basis that such 'laws' had been violated, each country then engaged in what can only be called acts of piracy, seizing American ships and their goods and crews at will. No amount of negotiation, bickering, pleading or threats by the Jefferson administration budged either nation from their entrenched positions.

Finally, in a desperate attempt to protect American seamen and hopefully teach both countries a lesson, Jefferson and Madison promoted a short term embargo on all American shipping. The hope was not so much to bring Britain and France economically to their knees as it was to help them realize their dependence on American goods, and that it would be in their best interest to treat the U.S. with greater respect. While many have characterized the embargo as a failure, it should be noted that it not only boosted domestic production and creation of the textile industry, but at the end of the day (after the War of 1812), the original goal of Jefferson and Madison was reached. Both Britain and France did eventually come to realize their need for American goods, and after a few more years of further wrangling came grudgingly to admit that their harsh measures needed to be eased. Unfortunately however, this acknowledgement was years in the making, since the intense hatred between the two nations made it difficult for them to see anything rationally.

In the waning months of Jefferson's presidency, it looked as if the embargo was a failure. American merchants were hurting badly. Jefferson was repeatedly urged to take action, to do something to fix the problem. It is significant and telling that the great and brilliant Jefferson did nothing. He knew that nothing he tried was likely to work, and that the embargo would expire under its own terms right as he left office.

It was against this backdrop that Madison assumed the presidency. As such, he inherited an impossible problem that had no solution. This was far worse than the temptation to go to war with Britain which was rebuffed by Washington while he was president, and the similar temptation toward war with France rebuffed by Adams while he was president. This was a problem decades in the making that had reached its peak while Jefferson was still president. There were pleas from all directions for action, but Madison knew that few actions were likely to succeed. In the end, as will be more fully explained in Chapter 5, Madison once again proved his genius in the course he took. And because of this, he finally and forever relieved the country of the ongoing disputes with Great Britain that had plagued the country since the Revolutionary War. In short, he accomplished what none of his illustrious predecessors had been able to accomplish--more stable relations with Britain.

Details of the War of 1812 and how many historians have got it all wrong about Madison's handling of the war are discussed more fully in chapter 5. As America's first war president, Madison proved himself more than equal to the task. His initial strategy of a quick invasion of Canada was brilliant, but was destroyed by timid and incapable generals. He correctly noted that New England's unwillingness to support the war was the major reason it dragged on so long. And in the end he attained a reasonable peace that entrenched the American presence on the continent far more firmly than had previously been the case. Madison was decisive and took prompt and effective action during the war. When the war ended, an era of unprecedented peace engulfed the country, largely due to his efforts. Why historians have failed to see this is truly a mystery.

After the end of the war in 1815, Madison was finally able to focus on domestic matters. One of his actions that may seem surprising was his support for re-charter of the national bank. He had vigorously opposed this bank when it was originally proposed by Hamilton, as being unconstitutional. The reasons for this switch, and a more detailed explanation of Madison's prophetic insights into financial matters, are treated more particularly in chapter 6.

Madison left the presidential chair in March, 1817, returning to his beloved Montpelier, Virginia for 19 years of peaceful solitude before his death in 1836. He was the last of the 'founding fathers' to pass on, and continued to apply his vigorous mind and active opinion in political and national matters until his death. He knew of and firmly criticized South Carolina's nullification of the federal tariff in 1832-33, and was aware of Andrew Jackson's fight over the national bank. He commented on these events, and continued to articulate his vision of federalism and the need for union at all costs.

One of his chief efforts was to counter the dangerous heresy of nullification and secession espoused by zealous southerners, who sometimes tried to use Madison and Jeffersons' Virginia and Kentucky Resolutions to support their cause. Madison did not hesitate to denounce such efforts, pointing out forcefully that nowhere in his Virginia Resolution did he encourage disunion. He described these resolutions simply for what they were--political statements by state legislatures expressing disapproval of an act of Congress--but not expressing disloyalty or unwillingness to comply with a law they disliked. For Madison, as always, it was the union first, last and foremost. A further consideration of these issues and of slavery in particular is discussed in Chapter 9.

Throughout his long life, Madison's views maintained a remarkable consistency and vision. Time and again his prophetic insights were vindicated by historical events. Time and again it was ultimately seen that the "radical" views he expressed were in fact not as radical as the views of those who opposed him, and that his measures were logical, sound and sure. His prophecies continue to this day to accomplish the same goals.

Madison truly saw our day. He saw our political struggles, our confusion about how to identify fundamental rights, our flirtations with unsound economic and military policies, our political bashing and mind-numbing wrangling over the trivial. And seeing these things, he provided a blueprint for us to follow to avoid being swallowed by a morass of senseless stupidity. His vision of government and the way it should work is as sound today as it was over 200 years ago.

And if we but have the sense to follow it, we will be saved from our own idiocy, and recover our dignity as a nation.

NOTES:

[1] Irving Brandt, The Fourth President: A Life of James Madison, 9 (1970).

[2] Gaillard Hunt ed., 1 The Writings of James Madison, 19 (1900-1910)(hereinafter "Hunt").

[3] Benjamin Rush, letter to his son of May 25, 1802, found in Saul K. Padover ed., The Complete Madison: His Basic Writings, 3 (1953).

[4] 1 Hunt at 11.

[5] Ibid at 16.

[6] 1 Annals of Congress 775 (1789)(Joseph Gales, ed, 1834).

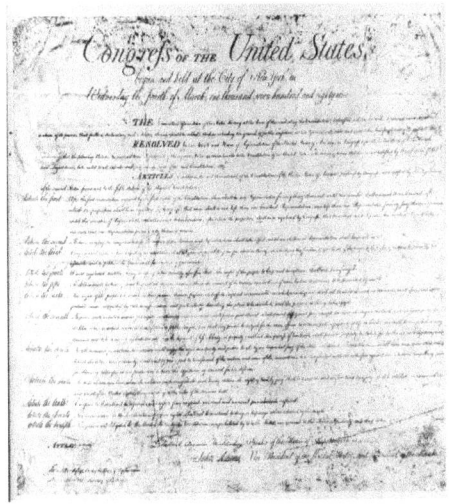

CHAPTER THREE
All About Rights and Where They Come From

Madison proposed the federal bill of rights in the House of Representatives in June, 1789, pushing for the new Congress to deal with rights as one of their top priorities. This new bill of rights would apply only to the federal government, not the states which already had their own bills of rights, since it would be another 100 years before the federal bill of rights came to be applied directly to the states under the 14th amendment. In calling for adoption of a bill of rights Madison was opposed by many of his fellow representatives who felt there were far more pressing matters to deal with than a mere listing of rights that none of them thought were in danger anyway, since rights seemed to be fully protected by the states. However, Madison proved his tenaciousness and political brilliance in continuing to push the issue until the new bill of rights was passed by Congress later that year, then sent to the states for ratification. In so doing, he secured his place in history not only as the 'Father of the Constitution,' but also as the 'Father of the Bill of Rights.'

It may therefore come as a profound shock for many to learn that Madison did not want a federal bill of rights at all, and would have greatly preferred not to be bothered with one. The simple reality is that he proposed the bill of rights for two reasons: (1) to pacify those who had only ratified the constitution with the promise that a federal bill of rights would be promptly adopted; and (2) to derail the call by opponents of the constitution for a second constitutional convention. In reality, both reasons were essentially the same, since everyone knew that those clamoring for a new constitutional convention were those who had opposed ratification due to the constitution's lack of a bill of rights. Madison knew that if a second convention occurred, the painstaking work in Philadelphia in the summer of 1787 would be lost, and the structure of the constitution would be seriously altered and damaged. Once again, he said it best in his own words: "I should be unwilling to see a door opened for a re-consideration of the whole structure of the government, for a re-consideration of the principles and the substance of the powers given; because I doubt, if such a door were opened, we should be very likely to stop at that point which would be safe to the Government itself."[7]

Accordingly, Madison pushed for the bill of rights for political reasons, not because he felt one was necessary. He knew that if he could quickly stop complaints about a lack of a bill of rights in the new constitution, then its enemies would be forced to change their tactics and to more openly pursue the structural changes they were really after--changes he was sure would not be adopted. And as usual, he was right. After the bill of rights was approved, calls for a second constitutional convention and for serious structural changes to the constitution grew fewer and fewer, and seemed more desperate and extreme. Eventually they died away altogether. This was because opponents of the constitution knew they had been outfoxed by Madison's bill of rights.

Indeed, they were aware of this even while the bill of rights were being debated. This is why many of them opposed his proposed wording of the bill of rights in 1789 as being inadequate.

But this effort also failed, again because of Madison's brilliance. In his bill of rights he carefully and specifically proposed only noncontroversial rights that no one would disagree with! As he stated, "nothing of a controvertible nature ought to be hazarded" in the proposed bill of rights, so that they would be easily approved. Most importantly, his proposal was "a conciliatory declaration of certain fundamental principles in favor of liberty, in a form not affecting the validity and plenitude of the ratification" of the constitution itself.[8]

All of this was a political battle of course, which really had nothing to do with rights. As for rights themselves, Madison personally did not believe that a written bill of rights was necessarily a good thing. While he never went so far as to say a bill of rights was worthless, and indeed agreed that it might serve some useful purpose, it was, for him, of little importance. Once again, his own words express his position best:

"[M]y own opinion has always been in favor of a bill of rights; provided it be so framed as not to imply powers not meant to be included in the enumeration. At the same time I have never thought the omission a material defect, nor been anxious to supply it even by subsequent amendment ... I have favored it because I supposed that it might be of use, and if properly executed could not be of disservice."[9]

He went on to explain why he didn't think a bill of rights was worth all the bother:

"I have not viewed it in an important light—1. because I conceive that in a certain degree . . .... the rights in question are reserved by the manner in which the federal powers are granted. 2 because there is great reason to fear that a positive declaration of some of the most essential rights could not be obtained in the requisite latitude. I am sure that the rights of conscience [religious freedom] in particular, if submitted to public definition would be narrowed much more than they are likely ever to be by an assumed power . . . . 3. because the limited powers of the federal Government and the jealousy of the subordinate [State] Governments, afford a security which has not existed in the State Governments, and exists in no other. 4. because experience proves the inefficacy of a bill of rights on those occasions when its control is most needed. Repeated violations of these parchment barriers have been committed by overbearing majorities in every state. In Virginia I have seen the bill of rights violated in every instance where it has been opposed to a popular current."[10]

This fourth concern is the most significant. In 1785 Madison had seen the Virginia legislature try to enact a law to use tax money to pay the clergy--a clear violation of the separation of church and state and religious freedom specified in Virginia's bill of rights. This proposed tax bill is discussed in greater detail in chapter 8. The bill failed to pass primarily because Madison and a few others opposed it so vigorously. Otherwise, the Virginia bill of rights would probably have been ignored. Indeed, as pointed out in the previous chapter, the federal first amendment right of free speech was ignored by the Federalist Congress when they passed the Alien and Sedition Acts in 1798. Once again, Madison's prophetic insight about the dubious workability of bills of rights has been vindicated by actual examples.

Madison's views on the questionable worth of a bill of rights did not change with time. As late as 1821, fully 32 years after he proposed the bill of rights and four years after he had ended his presidency and entered into retirement, he referred to the bill of rights as "those safe, if not necessary, and those politic, if not obligatory, amendments introduced in conformity to the known desires of the Body of the people."[11] In short, he never saw the bill of rights as essential, but was not opposed to it if it was carefully drafted. After all, it could provide some helpful service. But it's mere existence was no guarantee that rights would actually be protected.

Madison's somewhat negative view of a bill of rights, as little more than an ineffective 'paper barrier,' may give the impression that he did not care much for protecting the rights of the people. However, nothing could be further from the truth. Madison very firmly believed there was an effective way to protect individual rights from governmental abuses. This method was so vital to his thinking that he proposed it as the sixth resolution of his 'Virginia Plan' at the commencement of the Constitutional Convention in 1787. This was no afterthought, thrown out to satisfy the detractors who were crying for a bill of rights and threatening a second constitutional convention. Madison's plan to protect rights was more fundamental and more powerful. He desired for the federal legislature to retain the power to completely veto or 'negative' all acts by any of the state legislatures that might injure rights. Hence, his plan to protect rights pertained not just to federal but also to state abuses of rights, because Congress would be able to take direction action against a state's abuse of rights.

Some may think Madison's plan for Congress to have the power to veto state laws is extreme. However, many of the other delegates at the constitutional convention agreed with him. Indeed, his proposed 'legislative veto' was initially approved by vote of a majority of the delegates! But since this first vote was not binding, the issue came up for vote again, later on. This time it was defeated. Interestingly, the issue was voted on a third and final time toward the end of the convention. While it once more lost, the vote was closer this time.[12] Clearly, there were many that agreed with Madison that a federal 'legislative veto' was the best way to protect rights.

Indeed, consider for a moment the way things have evolved in the U.S. since the civil war when the federal government gained more power over the states. If Congress disagrees with any state law today, aren't they likely to pass a federal law of their own to counter it? Indeed, this has happened many times. Hence, Madison's proposed legislative veto is in fact largely followed by Congress today after all, except in cases of judicial activism where the Supreme Court has usurped this power. In short, since the civil war we have essentially adopted what Madison proposed originally. Unfortunately, as we shall see, the delegate's failure to adopt this measure in the beginning contributed to judicial activism that otherwise could possibly have been avoided.

Returning to Madison's proposal of the legislative veto in 1787, he summed up the need for it in these words: "an indefinite power to negative legislative acts of the states [was] absolutely necessary to a perfect system. Experience had evinced a constant tendency in the states to ... [among other things] oppress the weaker party within their jurisdictions."[13] The legislative veto would therefore be the chief method Congress could use to protect 'weaker parties' from loss of their rights at the hands of the majority. Madison saw this as a much more effective way to protect rights than creation of a written bill of rights that would apply only to the federal government, and furthermore would depend for its enforcement on judicial interpretations.

Madison greatly distrusted state legislatures and how they might exploit the innocent, or violate their rights. He was willing to put greater trust in the federal congress because of its larger diversity. As Madison explained in The Federalist No. 10, it would not be unusual at all for a faction to take control of smaller state governments. It was far less likely that a faction would gain control of the entire Congress, since it drew its membership from a diverse group of states. Madison stated in The Federalist No. 10 that "The influence of factious leaders may kindle a flame within their particular States, but will be unable to spread a general conflagration through the other States." This is because of the greater diversity to be found where there is a "greater number of citizens and extent of territory." Hence, the very size of a large republic would be the most effective tool for controlling the factions that arose within it.

Unfortunately for Madison, other members of the Constitutional Convention did not fully agree with his proposed legislative veto. They ultimately voted it down--but not completely. Instead, they replaced it with a 'judicial veto,' based on a list of things in Article 1 sections 9 and 10 that the federal Congress and the state legislatures could not do. Chief among these was the ban on bills of attainder, by which state legislatures could potentially deny the rights or take the property of citizens. If the federal or state governments enacted a bill of attainder or did any of the other prohibited things, the Supreme Court would 'veto' their law. As Governor Morris said, "a law that ought to be negatived will be set aside in the judiciary department and if that security should fail; may be repealed by a national law." Justice John Marshall characterized the list of prohibited actions in Article 1 section 10 as a 'bill of rights' in its own right.[14] Hence, the possibility of judicial activism by an over-seeing and over-zealous Supreme Court was born. In the beginning, as the Supreme Court exercised this power it usually curbed its zeal and did not seriously overstep its bounds. But with time the temptation for the judiciary to step into the legislative sphere and to recognize new rights not specifically listed in the constitution became too great, and zealous, judicial activism became a reality.

Madison did not like this idea about the 'judicial veto' very much, and for very sound reasons. Doing things in this way was frankly quite backward. Why allow a bad law to be passed that could more easily have been prevented? Then people must suffer from the oppressive law until it can be reviewed by the Supreme Court and (hopefully) overturned. Moreover, what would happen if the Court's interpretation was narrow? Wouldn't some aspects of the bad law continue? Once again, Madison said it best in his own words:

"It may be said that the Judicial authority, under our new system will keep the states within their proper limits, and supply the place of a negative on their laws. The answer is, that it is more convenient to prevent the passage of a law than to declare it void after it is passed."[15]

In so saying, Madison raised the very policy-making issue that is seen in judicial activism today. Judicial intervention in questions of rights can only come after a violation has occurred. The Supreme Court is aware that its decision is not limited to the case at hand, but will be considered binding law on all similarly situated persons in the future. It is also aware that its decision will override all legislation. In short, under such a system, courts could make policy decisions which are better left to the legislature. Madison disliked such a structure. For him it was abundantly obvious that the best branch of government to protect rights was the federal legislature, through a legislative veto.

Indeed, on another occasion, Madison commented pointedly about the dangers of judicial activism in respect to threatened rights. This comment was made in 1799, as part of his response to the 'Alien and Sedition' Acts which were enacted during the presidential administration of John Adams. In wording that is reminiscent of anti-terrorist legislation today, these acts allowed the president to deport 'dangerous' aliens, and criminalized certain public criticisms of the government. This naturally implicated the first amendment right of free speech. Because the authority to enact such restrictive laws was hard to find in the written constitution, some justified them on the basis that the constitution impliedly incorporated the British customary or 'common law,' and that the acts were made under the government's authority pursuant to the common law to protect itself. While some states had adopted the common law within their jurisdictions, the federal government had NEVER done so. It is not surprising therefore that Madison strongly disagreed with this assertion, and concluded that "the common law never was, nor by any fair construction ever can be, deemed a law for the American people." Madison was particularly firm that the Supreme Court should not interpret the common law as support for a constitutional right--which incidentally is exactly what the Supreme Court later did in the 1973 case of Roe v. Wade, in adopting what it characterized as the common law rule regarding abortion and a 'right of privacy.' Madison stated:

"Whether the common law be admitted as of legal or of constitutional obligation, it would confer on the judicial department a discretion little short of a legislative power ... [they would] decide what parts of the common law would, and what would not, be properly applicable to the circumstances of the United States. A discretion of this sort has always been lamented as incongruous and dangerous ... the power of the judges over the law would, in fact, erect them into legislators, and ... it would be impossible for the citizens to conjecture, either what was or would be law."[16]

This is as clear a warning against judicial activism as can be found. Madison was obviously against such activism by the Supreme Court, pursuant to which they would elevate themselves to handle matters of policy which were better left to the legislature.

Jefferson also was greatly concerned with judicial activism of this sort. In 1819 he expressed concern over the decisions of "unelected" judges who would view the constitution as "a mere thing of wax ... which they may twist and shape into any form they please." Other founders had similar concerns. Luther Martin, delegate to the constitutional convention from Maryland, noted at the convention in 1787 that "[a] knowledge of mankind, and of legislative affairs cannot be presumed to belong in a higher degree to the Judges than to the legislature."[17]

At this point, some may be inclined to criticize Madison for putting so much trust in the federal Congress. They may think it peculiar that Madison would distrust one legislature (of each state) so much that he would propose controlling them by way of a veto power in another legislative body (the federal Congress). While what Madison said in the Federalist number 10 is true, and the federal Congress is much less likely to be overcome by a faction than a state legislature, the possibility still exists that a faction could perhaps sweep the federal Congress as well.

Ever the pragmatist, Madison was fully aware of this and proposed a method to resolve it. He knew that even with the severe limitations on the power of Congress described in the Constitution, it still could possibly become controlled by a faction and abuse the rights of the people. That is why the eighth resolution of his 'Virginia Plan' proposed the formation of a 'council of revision', composed of the President and "a convenient number of the National Judiciary" who would have "authority to examine every act of the National Legislature before it should operate," with the power to veto any congressional act.[18] Significantly, such a veto could be overcome by Congress re-passing the law. This was the predecessor of the veto power, which was changed by the constitutional convention to rest solely with the President. It is noteworthy that this proposal--which involved the judiciary--required review of a law before it took effect, not afterward by way of a challenge to the law in the courts.

Of course, involving the Supreme Court in the veto of an act of Congress once more seems extreme to many in our day, since this would seem to suggest political activism by the court regarding proposed laws. But in fact, all that was really called for by Madison was what today is known as a 'declaratory judgment,' by which the court comments on the viability of a law. Declaratory judgments are commonly handed down by both state and federal courts today. Furthermore, when we consider the activism of the Supreme Court today, the genius of Madison's original proposal becomes even more apparent. As everyone knows, the Supreme Court is heavily motivated by political considerations. This is why every nomination of a new justice to the Supreme Court is such a political event. The Supreme Court frequently legislates for the entire country when it overturns state laws as 'unconstitutional.' As we saw above, the clearest example of this was the 1973 Roe v. Wade decision which effectively legalized abortion across all 50 states, contrary to dozens of state laws on the books. In short, having the Supreme Court participate in vetoing proposed legislation as Madison suggested is not as extreme a notion as it seems. And Madison's proposal had the added benefit of diffusing the veto power from the hands of a single man sitting in the presidential chair.

But most important of all, if the judiciary had been part of the veto process as Madison envisioned, the Supreme Court's assumption of an activist position on political matters would have been largely diffused, at least in respect to federal laws. This is because of the way a combined veto power of the president and judiciary would have impacted both proposed laws and later court cases. Rather than hand down a decision after legislation had become binding law, the court would have joined with the president in vetoing proposed bad laws before they could take effect. This would have a twofold impact: (1) it would encourage Congress to revise the law in a way that would be more acceptable and would not later be found unconstitutional; and (2) it would naturally decrease the number of later lawsuits even in respect to such laws. Most tellingly, the Supreme Court would have found it very difficult at a later date to declare a law of Congress unconstitutional that it had previously failed to veto. What this would effectively mean is that, if this 'council of revision' plan of presidential/supreme court vetoing had been adopted, the Supreme Court would rarely declare a law of congress to be unconstitutional thereby legislating for the entire country as it now often does. The only time this would likely happen is where Congress overrode a presidential/Supreme Court veto by 2/3s vote, and enacted their proposed law anyway--truly a rare event.

But there is more. If this model of judicial participation in the veto power had been adopted, it is most likely that many states would have adopted it in their state constitutions as well. Consequently, many bad state laws would also be vetoed by a combination of the state supreme court and the state governor before taking effect. This again would reduce the number of state cases ultimately appealed to the US Supreme Court and declared unconstitutional by that body. And this would consequently have reduced the likelihood of the Supreme Court becoming a law unto itself.

But of course, that does not mean the Supreme Court would be utterly stopped from being activist. Taking the Roe v. Wade decision as an example, the Texas Supreme Court and governor may have felt the Texas abortion law was acceptable, and not vetoed it. The US Supreme Court may have later ruled it to be unconstitutional just like they did in 1973. It would seem then that Madison's idea would not solve this aspect of judicial activism involving review of state laws, and would not have prevented the activist Roe decision.

The short answer to this is that such a review takes too narrow a view of Madison's ideas about rights. He had more ideas to curb judicial activism of the Supreme Court than just judicial participation in the veto power. If all of his ideas had been properly implemented, the Roe v. Wade decision could never have occurred.

To better understand Madison's inspired ideas about rights and about curbing Supreme Court activism, we must come to comprehend his ideas about the Ninth Amendment and the unenumerated rights it referred to. We must also come to understand his ideas about the binding nature of the original intent of the founding fathers, and how their intent should govern the Supreme Court's constitutional interpretations. Once we understand his ideas on these topics, we will more readily see how the Roe v. Wade decision never could have happened, and why proper application of Madison's vision would resolve the judicial activism of the Supreme Court that plagues the country today.

NOTES:

[7] 1 Annals of Congress, 433 (1789)(Joseph Gales ed., 1834). Madison's speech presenting the proposed Bill of Rights was given in the House of Representatives on June 8, 1789. Ibid at 431-42.

[8] 5 Hunt at 226-27, 406 (1904).

[9] Ibid at 271.

[10] Ibid at 271-72. A primary example was the 1785 attempt by the Virginia legislature to enact a tax to pay the clergy. Madison strongly opposed the effort, which therefore failed. See 2 Hunt at 183-91.

[11] 9 Hunt at 75 (1910).

[12] 3 Hunt at 55, 127 (1902); 4 Hunt at 286-288 (1903).

[13] 3 Hunt at 121 (1902).

[14] For Morris' comments see 3 Hunt at 449; Marshall's statement is found in Fletcher v. Peck, 10 U.S. (6 Cranch) 87, 138 (1810).

[15] 5 Hunt at 26-27.

[16] 6 Hunt at 380-381 (1906).

[17] For Jefferson's comments, see Paul Leicester Ford ed., 10 The Writings of Thomas Jefferson, 141 (1899); for Luther Martin's comments, see 4 Hunt at 26 (1903).

[18] 3 Hunt at 19.

CHAPTER FOUR
The Purpose of the Ninth Amendment, and the Concept of Original Intent

We saw above that Madison felt a bill of rights could only be acceptable "provided it be so framed as not to imply powers not meant to be included in the enumeration." In other words, he was concerned that if a right was not specifically enumerated and listed in the bill of rights, this would imply that the federal government had the power to deny that right. Madison was far from alone in having this concern. James Jackson from Georgia, one of the members of the House of Representatives when Madison presented his proposed bill of rights, stated the problem quite well:

"There is a maxim in law, and it will apply to bills of rights, that when you enumerate exceptions, the exceptions operate to the exclusion of all circumstances that are omitted; consequently, unless you except every right from the grant of power, those omitted are inferred to be resigned to the discretion of the Government."[19]

Madison repeated this concern in his speech in 1789 when he presented his proposed bill of rights for Congress to consider. In this speech he listed a number of good and bad points about having a bill of rights, but only expressed serious concern about this one issue. Here are his words:

"It has been objected also against a bill of rights, that, by enumerating particular exceptions to the grant of power, it would disparage those rights which were not placed in that enumeration, and it might follow by implication, that those rights which were not singled out, were intended to be assigned into the hands of the general government, and were consequently insecure. *This is one of the most plausible arguments I have ever heard urged against the admission of a bill of rights into this system.*"[20]

With his usual brilliance, Madison proposed a solution to this problem. He wanted to include among the new amendments the following language: "The exceptions here or elsewhere in the constitution, made in favor of particular rights, shall not be so construed as to diminish the just importance of other rights retained by the people; or as to enlarge the powers delegated by the constitution; but either as actual limitations of such powers, or as inserted merely for greater caution."[21] The reference to "greater caution" reiterates Madison's belief that a bill of rights was not really necessary but was more of a cautionary statement, since the rights it listed were so fundamental that they would be protected by the government in any event. Indeed, the experience of Australia confirms this. To this day, Australia has no bill of rights, yet fundamental rights such as speech or religion continue to be protected there essentially the same as in America. On the other hand, the Peoples Republic of China, Cuba and North Korea all have bills or declarations of rights, which are handily ignored. The existence of a bill of rights has not seemed to change rights protections in these various countries.

Congress generally agreed with Madison's proposal, but changed and shortened the wording to what we today know as the Ninth Amendment: "The enumeration in the

Constitution of certain rights shall not be construed to deny or disparage others retained by the people."

The concept is simple. The people retain more rights than are listed in the bill of rights, and those unlisted or unenumerated rights deserve just as much protection as the listed ones. What is fascinating about this concept is how it has come to be viewed today. Modern judges and scholars looking at the Ninth Amendment fixate on a problem with that amendment of their own creation--a 'problem' that was not even perceived as one by Madison or his contemporaries, since the plain understanding of the Ninth Amendment was so overwhelmingly clear to them. The 'problem' is this: How are we to identify what these extra rights are?

This brings us to the 1973 case of Roe v. Wade, and the decision by the Supreme Court to deny the rights of the unborn (fulfilling Madison's prophecy of government assuming power to deny unlisted rights) and creation of a new thing called 'a woman's right of privacy,' which was said to include her right to obtain an abortion. Interestingly, the 1973 Supreme Court did not derive this right from the Ninth Amendment, but rather from the common law based on rather vague 'due process' language in the Fourteenth Amendment, thereby further confusing and confounding where this alleged right supposedly came from. It should be noted that the British common law rule regarding abortion was merely a rule of evidence, which denied the right to an abortion after evidence that the child was moving and therefore alive. Conclusive evidence in that day could not be offered until roughly 4 months into pregnancy. The Roe court seized on this time while handily ignoring the evidentiary nature of the rule, and declared that 4 months, or the second trimester, was the point at which abortions could start to be protected by state laws. However, when understood as the simple law of evidence that it was, under the common law abortions should be illegal under state law from approximately the 25th day after conception--or roughly the time a woman realizes she is pregnant--since that is the time a fetal heartbeat is detectable today, which is undeniable evidence of movement and life.

For Madison and the founding generation, there was no question where rights were derived, including all unlisted rights that could come under the Ninth Amendment. It certainly wasn't from the common law, which Madison characterized as being full of "incongruities, barbarisms, and bloody maxims."[22] Even today, the common law is considered as the lowest form of law, and every lawyer knows that it can easily be overturned by any act of the legislature or any decision by a judge. On the contrary, Madison knew that true rights came from natural law, also known as the law of nature. These were the highest form of rights, higher even than constitutional law, and could not be overturned by any legislature, court or body of men. The best known example of such an unlisted, unchangeable natural law right was the one stated eloquently by Thomas Jefferson in the Declaration of Independence. He said that under "the laws of nature and of nature's God ... whenever any form of government becomes destructive ... it is the right of the people to alter or abolish it, and to institute new government." The right to rebel against unjust and destructive government is not listed in the bill of rights, but is an eternal and unchangeable natural right retained by the people.

Interestingly, most modern scholars who have studied the Ninth Amendment agree that the rights the amendment was intended to protect are those derived from natural law.[23] They still flounder however in trying to identify these rights, rather than to follow the incredibly simple and obvious expedient--generally followed or at least acknowledged in every other case of constitutional interpretation today but this--of deriving such rights from the view of the founding generation themselves.

In other words, it is *the founding generation's views* of natural law that was to be incorporated into the Ninth Amendment, and the rights it was meant to cover were rights *they* understood it would cover. This was certainly Madison's understanding. He frequently referred to the Constitution with its bill of rights as a social compact, or in other words, as essentially a contract formulated by and among the American people. The Ninth Amendment was an open-ended reference to rights not listed, but known to exist. In contract law if there is ever an open-ended reference to something not listed that is to be part of the contract (which is known in legal terms as an 'incorporation by reference clause'), the terms to be incorporated must be in existence and acknowledged at the time the open-ended provision is made part of the contract! No contract lawyer in his right mind would create an open-ended reference to rights in a contract with the intention that later interpreters of the contract could change those previously incorporated and understood terms at their whim. Yet that is exactly the bizarre way that most scholars and judges view the Ninth Amendment today.

Returning again to the Roe v. Wade decision, if the Supreme Court had been doing its job correctly it would have acknowledged that any unlisted right that it 'found' would have to be derived solely from the Ninth Amendment rather than the Fourteenth Amendment, since that is the Ninth Amendment's job. In connection with this, they would have also been constrained to acknowledge that since the Ninth Amendment was essentially an 'incorporation by reference clause,' any such right derived from it would have to be a natural law right acknowledged by the founding generation in their day. Some people try to object to this clear and simple reality on the basis that there are supposedly "new rights" that have come into being in modern times that were not contemplated in the founder's day. This is utter nonsense. Rights are moral issues, and the founding generation dealt with such issues at length and were extremely familiar with them. Modern technology does not create new rights anymore than it creates morals. Look at any of the rights debated today, and you will see that they or something like unto them were known to the founders. The most telling example of this is abortion, since this practice was well known in the founder's day, and many of the founders spoke against it (none spoke in favor of it).

To be more specific, John Adams spoke against abortion in praising the Greek reformer Lycurgus and his refusal to countenance such a practice. Jefferson spoke against it as a practice that would only be engaged in by uncivilized savages. Hamilton spoke against it, when he opposed a 'concealment law' in New York, under which an unmarried woman was automatically assumed guilty of murdering a child of hers who was found dead unless she could offer proof to the contrary. Hamilton opposed this law because it reversed the presumption that a person is innocent until proven guilty, but his comments make it clear that if proof were shown that a woman had aborted her child she should be prosecuted for murder. Jefferson made similar comments about Virginia's 'concealment law.' Benjamin Rush, signer of the Declaration of Independence and a physician, also spoke against abortion in clear terms, as did James Wilson.[24]

As if this were not enough, every one of the natural law writers relied on and believed in by the founding generation, and on whom the founders based their concepts of natural law, wrote specifically and pointedly against abortion as well! In order to better grasp this reality, it is first helpful to identify the natural law writers relied on by the founding generation. Alexander Hamilton probably provided the best list when he said in his response to British sympathizer Samuel Seabury in 1775, "[a]pply yourself, without delay, to the study of the law of nature. I would recommend to your perusal, Grotius, Pufendorf, Locke, Montesquieu, and Burlemaqui." James Otis in his speeches before the revolution often cited Pufendorf, Grotius, Barbeyrac and Burlemaqui. James Wilson in his lecture on 'The Natural Rights of the Individual' referred to these same natural law writers.[25] It is well known to this day that John Locke was probably the most famous of these, and was heavily relied on by the founding generation. Thomas Jefferson's Declaration of Independence was heavily 'Lockean' in its tone.

These natural law writers who the founders read, followed and revered, were quite open and firm in condemning abortion as a violation of the law of nature. For example, John Locke included abortion on a list of wrong and unacceptable actions: "not to kill another man; not to know more women than one; not to procure abortion; not to expose their children; not to take from another what is his ..." In addition, Locke said that "the body of an embryo, dying in the womb, may be very little, not the thousandth part of an ordinary man. For since from the first conception and beginning of formation, it has life."[26] This is an incredibly strong statement about the need to protect life from the moment of conception.

Other natural law writers were in agreement. For example, Montesquieu stated "There is among savages another custom ... it is the cruel practice of abortion to which their women are addicted, in order that pregnancy may not render them distasteful to their husbands." No doubt basing his comments on this statement, Thomas Jefferson also condemned abortion as a practice that only an uncivilized savage would engage in. Grotius and Burlemaqui both stated that unborn children should be considered as already born, whenever their advantage was in question.[27]

Samuel von Pufendorf was the most prolific of the natural law writers on this subject. For example, in speaking of those who have no rights because they are not yet "a part of the world," he stated: "[n]ow by him who is not yet a part of the world we understand one who has not yet been conceived, not one who is still in the womb." He also said, "Obligation has also been enjoined upon parents by the law of nature, that not merely shall they not destroy by abortion the offspring conceived within their flesh, nor expose it, nor put it to death after it has been brought into the light of day; but also that they shall supply it with nourishment (one or both of them, just as they have agreed in the marriage pact), until it can conveniently support itself."[28]

Some today don't like to hear such things. They like to pretend that abortion is a modern issue, somehow made more acceptable by technology that terminates the fetus more quickly. But there is no logic to such a position. Abortion is abortion, whether it occurred in 1787 or occurs today. There is no legal or logical basis for finding a woman's 'right' to an abortion under the constitution, since under the Ninth Amendment's incorporation of natural law the opposite is true!

Yet many still struggle with this. The idea that Ninth Amendment natural law rights are to be solely found based on the views of the founding generation is uncomfortable for many, in spite of their reliance on the founders for the constitution they profess to cherish. They prefer to view the constitution as an open-ended document that can be re-interpreted to mean something different than its founders intended. This leads us to the topic of 'original intent.' For decades judges and legal scholars have debated whether general, undefined or ambiguous terms in the Constitution are to be interpreted according to the understanding and intent of the founders, or according to our own modern whims. The commentary and scholarship on this topic are voluminous, and it is not the goal of this book to review the literature on the subject, other than to point out one amazing fact--the scholars and judges that have reviewed this issue have largely ignored what Madison said about it!

And once more, we see the prophetic genius of Madison, since this was far too significant an issue to be ignored. He clearly spoke in favor of reliance on the original intent of the founders, and that succeeding generations were bound by that intent. Madison articulated his ideas on the subject in response to a letter in 1790 he received from his good friend Jefferson. Jefferson suggested the theory that, since mortality rates at that time resulted in a turnover of the majority of the population every 19 years, and since he felt that a living generation could bind only itself, all governments and laws were subject to repeal and re-creation by each generation every 19 years.[29] Madison disagreed, citing a number of reasons new generations owed allegiance to the government and the laws made by their predecessors as those laws were understood by the prior generation. Madison first identified three classes of laws: fundamental constitutions, permanent laws, and temporary laws. He then articulated compelling reasons why each category of laws and its original interpretation should endure past 19 years--reasons that frequently crossed the line to apply to each of the three categories of law he had identified.

For example, Madison said "would not a government so often revised become too mutable and novel to retain that share of prejudice in its favor [ie, following of tradition or precedent] which is a salutary aid to the most rational government?" In other words, if the original intent of the founders has no meaning and the Supreme Court is able to revise and modify the understanding of what "rights" can be derived under the constitution, this will undermine the stability of rational government itself. Madison's next comment then highlighted this point even more: "would not such a periodical revision engender pernicious factions that might not otherwise come into existence; and agitate the public mind more frequently and more violently than might be expedient?"[30] What a tremendously prophetic statement on what happens every time a new case on abortion or contraception or gay marriage or any other spinoff of the so-called "right of privacy" comes up to the Supreme Court for review? Clearly the public mind is agitated on these issues, and factions both for and against the various positions take to the streets to espouse their views. This only occurs because the various groups wrongly assume the question is an open one, rather than one in which only the founding generation's original intent matters.

But Madison wasn't through. He then specifically articulated the need for adherence to the original intent of the founders--even after they were long dead--to govern the interpretation of laws. He said: "The [governmental] improvements made by the dead [ie, the laws and rights articulated by the founding generation] form a debt against the living, who take the benefit of them. This debt cannot be otherwise discharged than by a proportionate obedience to the will of the Authors of the improvements." In short, we today must obey the original intent of the founding generation. What an incredibly clear statement in favor of original intent, and the binding nature of the founding generation's views on natural law rights!

Madison then commented that even the founders' temporary laws and their understanding of them needed to endure beyond 19 years, since otherwise "all the rights depending on positive laws, that is most of the rights of property would become absolutely defunct, and the most violent struggles ensue." This is a fascinating and clear statement by Madison that there is a difference between unchangeable natural laws--such as those protected by the Ninth Amendment and the bill of rights--and the "positive laws" created by men, most of which relate to property transfers and ownership. If even these lower level property laws were subject to re-interpretation, revision and abolition every 19 years, then "the most violent struggles [would] ensue between the parties interested in reviving [the old property laws] and those interested in reforming the antecedent state of property [laws]."[31] It is only too obvious that if even temporary property laws must be consistently interpreted according to the will and intent of their drafters, so must the founding generation's understanding of the natural law rights of the people.

As for Jefferson, it appears that he tended to believe the same as Madison on original intent. In 1823 he stated that "On every question of construction, [let us] carry ourselves back to the time when the Constitution was adopted, recollect the spirit manifested in the debates, and instead of trying what meaning may be squeezed out of the text, or invented against it, conform to the probable one in which it was passed." In short, just like Madison he felt constitutional interpretation should be bound by the intent of the founding generation. It should further be noted that even in his earlier '19-year' discussion Jefferson was very clear on the point that even if each new generation created its government anew, *it would be bound by the unchangeable requirements of natural law* in creating that government.[32]

Again, some are troubled at committing ourselves to following the intent of the founding generation who are long since gone, and who were not acquainted with the modern world. However, the truth is that the founders wrote extensively on a plethora of subjects that cover every moral contingency, even including the moral aspects related to changes from modern technology if we simply analogize with the terminology of their day. There are really no moral issues they were not aware of or dealt with, since our modern legal conundrums (such as abortion, the right of privacy, the right to die, the right of parents to educate their children, etc., etc.) are not based on technology but on morality. And if there is ever any doubt as to what the founders thought these rights are, resort can be made to the numerous natural law writers relied on by the founders such as John Locke, Grotius, Burlemaqui, Montesquieu and Pufendorf.

Some enterprising students of Madison may at this point argue that Madison was against original intent, citing as evidence his reluctance to publish his notes of the

Constitutional Convention which would have guided constitutional interpretation, and also citing a statement he made in 1821. This 1821 statement has been frequently quoted by opponents of original intent, and therefore needs to be clarified:

"As a guide in expounding and applying the provisions of the constitution, the debates and incidental decisions of the convention can have no authoritative character ... the legitimate meaning of the instrument must be derived from the text itself; or if a key is to be sought elsewhere, it must be not in the opinions or intentions of the body which planned and proposed the constitution, but in the sense attached to it by the people in their respective state conventions where it received all the authority which it possesses."[33]

Those who quote this passage in an effort to establish Madison's opinion against original intent almost always fail to mention a number of important and highly enlightening facts that clarify his meaning. First was that the motivation for his writing the statement at all was because some notes of the convention written by Robert Yates had just barely been published, which purported to show Madison's opinions at the convention in a questionable light. Madison logically reminded us that the convention debates were intended to be secret, so that members could alter their opinions over time and change their votes. As such, deriving an original intent from the war of words and widely varying opinions of the delegates is problematic to say the least. It is therefore not surprising that Madison sought to distance constitutional interpretation from the debates of the convention delegates.

Second and more importantly, Madison included the quoted statement as a footnote in a letter that expounded on the idea of original intent in greater detail, and which significantly clarified what he meant by it. In the letter he first noted that the opinions of individual delegates were not always a good guide in constitutional interpretation because "it sometimes happened that opinions as to a particular modification or a particular power of the government had a conditional reference to others which combined therewith would vary the character of the whole." In other words, opinions in notes did not give the whole picture, and were not entirely reliable. He then made the following statement, which directly confirms his idea that subsequent generations are bound by the interpretation and understanding of the constitution by his generation of Americans. The emphasis in the quote was made by Madison in the original: "But whatever might have been the opinions entertained in forming the Constitution, it was the duty of all to support it in its true meaning as understood *by the nation* at the time of its ratification." Could he have been any more clear? This is simply a reiteration of his quote above that subsequent generations are indebted to strictly follow the understandings of *the founding generation.* Madison then stated that "departures from the true and fair construction of the instrument have always given me pain, and always experienced my opposition when called for." He was particularly wary of "the abandonment of all rules of expounding it [such as abandonment of the rule of original intent], which were capable of transforming it into something very different from its legitimate character."[34]

At roughly this same time Madison wrote another letter which further clarified his thoughts on the issue. This letter emphasizes his point--clearly articulated in the 1821 quote above--that the best interpretive guide for the constitution was the sense of the nation as a whole as expressed in their ratifying conventions, rather than the opinions of individual convention delegates. In other words, interpretation was to be grounded on the views of the founding generation! He stated: "I entirely concur in the propriety of resorting to the sense in which the Constitution was accepted and ratified by the nation. In that sense alone it is the legitimate Constitution. And if that be not the guide in expounding it, there can be no security for a consistent and stable [interpretation]." Once again, how could he have been more clear? As noted above, abortion, gay marriage and a "right of privacy" was NOT something that particular generation of Americans believed in. If we abandon the understanding of the founding generation, we have no security, stability or consistency, and will drift wherever the wind blows us. Indeed, this is exactly what we have seen happen in recent years regarding abortion. But Madison wasn't through. He then articulated a concern about interpretation of the constitution which greatly clarified what he meant when he said it should be interpreted by its 'text,' and which showed that he never intended a 'textual' or word-based interpretation to override the intention and understanding of the founding generation. The concern he expressed here was again highly prophetic, since the Supreme Court has done precisely what he describes here as being unacceptable:

"If the meaning of the text be sought in the changeable meaning of the words composing it, it is evident that the shape and attributes of the Government must partake of the changes to which the words and phrases of all living languages are constantly subject. What a metamorphosis would be produced in the code of law if all its ancient phraseology were to be taken in its modern sense."[35]

Finally and most compellingly of all, it must be remembered that the issues most hotly debated about the constitution at the time of its ratification had to do with structural matters and the state/federal relationship. While rights were called for, their substance was hardly debated at all by the founders! More specifically, the individual rights listed in the bill of rights proposed by Madison in 1791 were hardly even debated. This is because the view of rights by the founding generation was remarkably cohesive and like-minded, and this view included not only the listed rights in the first eight amendments, but the natural law rights incorporated by reference in the Ninth Amendment. While structural state/federal constitutional matters (regarding which the founder's intent may be less than fully clear) do occasionally arise for interpretation today, by far the most hotly contested and divisive issues relate to rights. Yet the founding generation was remarkably clear about rights. If we would but follow their understanding and view of natural law rights, we would not be debating these issues at all.

One final note needs to be made. As articulated in the last chapter, among the many principles espoused by Madison, one which he perhaps held most dear, was that protection of rights was something best accomplished by the federal legislature rather than the federal courts. This was expressed in his idea of the legislative veto. Even if we could somehow ignore the overwhelmingly obvious duty we have to be bound by and follow the rights-understanding of the founding generation, we should not countenance or tolerate judicial mandates that essentially 'create' new rights, or mandate rights across the country without the vote of the people. If people today are unwilling to acknowledge and follow the natural law rights of the founding generation, they should at least follow Madison's prophetic counsel and acknowledge the need for rights questions to be decided by their legislators rather than their judges. This can be accomplished by a constitutional amendment which gives to the federal congress the final say in rights questions, after the Supreme Court has issued its rulings.[36] The only limitation to this would be in respect to rights of the criminally accused, which need to remain under the protective umbrella of the judiciary. Such procedural rights relating to the criminally accused include the right to habeas corpus, to a jury trial, to call witnesses, and to not be compelled to testify against oneself. These types of procedural criminal protections are best left with the judiciary since if the legislature were to control them, their actions could amount to an unconstitutional "bill of attainder," under which the legislature may act judicially to criminally punish a person or group that it believes deserves punishment, without the protection of due process of law. But other rights, including but not limited to the alleged right of (sexual) privacy, the right to die, the right to work and the right to educate one's children, are best left to the legislature. In short, the judiciary is best at overseeing procedural protections for criminally accused persons, while the legislature is best at resolving disputed policy issues.

In sum, Madison foresaw the difficulty we would have in protecting and dealing with rights. He preferred legislative control of rights questions by way of a legislative veto, rather than giving the judiciary this power by way of a judicial veto. While he was initially overruled in his day, the essence of his legislative veto idea is essentially practiced by Congress today, except where the Supreme Court has usurped this authority. Meanwhile, as for the judicial veto, Madison prophetically saw that the British common law should never be the basis of federal court decisions. He further indicated that the

Ninth Amendment was intended to protect natural rights as they were understood in his day, and that future generations were obligated to continue to recognize the rights-understanding of the founders. If we would but follow Madison's prophetic lead on these issues today, the ongoing drama of judicial activism and recognition of nonexistent 'rights' that are contrary to those recognized by the founding generation would become things of the past.

NOTES:

[19] 1 Annals of Congress 460 (1789)(Joseph Gales, ed, 1834).

[20] 5 Hunt at 384 (emphasis added).

[21] Ibid at 378.

[22] 6 Hunt at 380.

[23] See e.g. Bennett B. Patterson, The Forgotten Ninth Amendment, 19 (1955); Daniel A. Farber, Retained by the People: The 'Silent' Ninth Amendment and the Constitutional Rights Americans Don't Know They Have 8 (2007); Randy Barnett, "The Ninth Amendment: It Means What it Says," 85 Tex. L. Rev. 2 (2006).

[24] John Adams statement can be found at Charles Francis Adams ed., 4 The Works of John Adams, 549 (1851). Jefferson's statement

about savages is found at 3 Ford at 153, and his statement about the concealment law of Virginia is found at John P. Foley ed., The Jeffersonian Cyclopedia, at 598 (1900). Hamilton's comments are found in Harold C. Syrett & Jacob E. Cooke eds., 4 The Papers of Alexander Hamilton, at 39 (1962). The Benjamin Rush statement is found in Dagovert D. Runes ed., The Selected Writings of Benjamin Rush, at 151 (1947). James Wilson's comments are found at Robert G. McCloskey ed., 2 The Works of James Wilson, at 597 (1967).

[25] For Hamilton's comment, see 1 Syrett & Cooke at 86. For James Otis' comments see John Adams and Jonathon Sewell, Novanglus and Massachusettensis: or Political Essays Published in the Years 1774 and 1775, at 230 (1968)(1819). It should be noted that Barbeyrac was primarily a translator of the works of Grotius and Pufendorf. For the reference to James Wilson see McCloskey at 585 et seq.

[26] G. Knaller & T.A. Dean eds., 1 The Works of John Locke in Nine Volumes, at 48, 311 (12th ed., 1824).

[27] For Montesquieu's statement, see Montesquieu, The Persian Letters, at 218 (1721)(1901 Herat ed.). Jefferson's statement is found in 3 Ford, at 153. The statement by

Burlemaqui is found at Jean-Jacques Burlemaqui, The Principles of Natural and Political Law, at 84-85 (Petter Korkman ed., 2006)(1747). The statement by Grotius is found at Hugo Grotius, Introduction to Dutch Jurisprudence, Ch. III, sec. 4, XVL.

[28] Samuel Pufendorf, 2 Eight Books on Natural Rights, at 657 (C.H. Oldfather & W.A. Oldfather eds., 1934)(1688); Samuel Pufendorf, 2 The Elements of Universal Jurisprudence, at 283 (W.A. Oldfather ed., 1931)(1660).

[29] Jefferson's explanation of this idea is found in 5 Ford at 117-119.

[30] 5 Hunt at 438-439.

[31] Ibid at 439.

[32] Jefferson's 1823 statement is found in 10 Ford, at 231. His reference to natural law is found in 5 Ford at 119-121.

[33] 9 Hunt at 72.

[34] Ibid at 74.

[35] Ibid at 191.

[36] For a more detailed discussion of such a proposed amendment, see my article: Duane L. Ostler, "Legislative Oversight of a Bill of Rights: A Way to Rectify Judicial Activism,"

90(5) Washington University Law Review 1581 (2013).

CHAPTER FIVE
America's First War President

James Madison was our first war president. How he handled matters of foreign policy and war is very telling. With full knowledge and respect of both the constitutional power and constitutional limits of the executive branch, he used his office to pursue a foreign policy that he felt was best for the nation. However, he never overstepped his bounds to intrude on the rights of Congress, even when he strongly disagreed with their action (or inaction, as it turned out). He firmly and consistently negotiated for peace, but was not afraid of going to war. He ignored how foreign policy could harm him politically (it nearly cost him the election of 1812), and resisted the urges of many around him to use the power of his office to silence those who disagreed with him, as John Adams had done in agreeing to the Alien and Sedition acts of 1798. He later refused to take action against those in the country who openly and even treasonously failed to support the war. He bravely stood silent while he was pilloried in the press with a level of viciousness unparalleled in American history. He did his best to find competent war generals, suffering at the hands of incompetents in a way that strongly resembles what Abraham Lincoln later experienced. He didn't divert blame when it was thrown his way, even though in almost every case it was unjustified. And at the end of the day, after having firmly stood his ground, he attained a level of peace that had eluded all of his predecessors in the presidential chair, and left his successor, James Monroe, as leader in one of the most peaceful eras of good feelings that the country has ever seen. In all of these endeavors, Madison showed what it was to be a truly great president, to honor the constitution, to stand for what was right even when heavily criticized, and to unflinchingly fulfill his duty. His example could well be followed today.

It was characteristic of Madison that he was never overly concerned with negative public opinion about himself. He was about as un-Nixonlike in this respect as it is possible for a person to be. As noted in a previous chapter, Washington Irving characterized Madison as a "withered little apple-john" given his small frame and diminutive size. Madison remained silent. The Federalists, which were the opposing political party, schizophrenically characterized him as both the sole cause of dragging a reluctant country to war and the puppet of congressmen in his party who dragged him unwillingly into war. Madison didn't take their bait, but followed a steady, consistent course of policy in an impossible situation. He was accused of using foreign policy and the possibility of war to increase his chances for reelection (something commonly heard today in presidential reelection campaigns), even though the declaration of war came at the worst possible time for his reelection chances. He was pilloried as having been outfoxed and cleverly deceived by Napoleon notwithstanding his constant and repeated statements of distrust of the French. In short, there was simply no accusation that anyone failed to raise against Madison. Most of the time he remained silent while plodding forward. When he did respond, it was not as a wounded, defensive target, but with simple, straightforward comments that justified his position.

Perhaps we can gain some perspective of the difficulty of what he faced by reviewing the impossible situation when he took office in 1809. By then, Britain and France had been at war for several years. Each had enacted restrictive trade laws, making it illegal for any nation to bring goods into the port of the other. America was caught in the crossfire of these policies, which was particularly troubling since the fledgling American economy depended so heavily on trade with these two countries. Indeed, America was the chief trading partner of the British and French prior to their restrictive trade laws. Each country resented American goods flowing into the other country, and tried to stop it. Britain did more than that. It started 'impressing' American seamen from American ships on the high seas, ostensibly on the basis that they were deserter English sailors. As one historian noted, "the European conflict subjected the country to unbearable humiliation. American seamen were impressed onto British warships which aggressively patrolled the American coast. England and France alike seized and confiscated American ships and cargoes. Aggravating Britain's conduct were commercial restrictions designed to reduce the United States to semi-colonial status."[37]

After years of attempted and failed negotiations with each country to prod them into lifting their restrictions, Jefferson had met this crisis with an unpopular embargo. The concept was simple--if neither country would permit trade with the other while still seeking it for themselves, they both would be equally denied. But such an effort took a heavier toll on America than it did on Britain or France. For it to work in those countries, it needed to be in place for several years, during which time the entire American economy might be ruined. In short, it was a good try at a nonmilitary solution, but it failed.

As Jefferson's term ended it is notable that he was continually urged to take a different course, to try to end the stalemate. He did nothing. This is significant. Surely the vaunted genius Jefferson did not want to leave his legacy tainted by this problem! Surely if there was a solution, he would have put it in place, thereby ensuring prosperity for his country and a lasting legacy of his genius. But he did nothing. And the simple reality is, he did nothing because there was nothing that could be done.

That is precisely the impossible situation that Madison inherited when he took office. Every effort at negotiation and economic sanction had already been tried. All had failed. The situation was as bad as ever, and the need for a solution was drastic. There could hardly be a more impossible problem to solve. Yet within six years, Madison had solved it. The process of doing so however was not easy.

Add to this that Madison's own party during this time was split. While many supported him and his policies, many did not. Consistently over the crucial six years until this ghastly foreign policy crisis was resolved, congress tended to deny Madison what he asked for rather than give it to him. This is particularly true of military preparation for war. As early as 1809, the year he took office, and fully 3 years before war was declared, Madison strongly urged congress to bolster the military and increase defense spending. They not only refused, but decreased it instead. Then naturally, when war later eventuated, Madison got all the blame for the lack of military preparedness.

And what of the war itself? Was Madison a fool for getting into it, knowing that the military was seemingly unprepared and that all three of his predecessors had refused war even when it was called for? Many historians have said he was. They are wrong. By 1809, Madison knew the country could handle a war if it had to--and it had to! But such a war could not have been successfully pursued at an earlier time. Consider for example a few significant and overwhelmingly obvious facts about the war of

1812 that supposedly enlightened historians have overlooked:

- The Revolutionary War could not have been won without a powerful foreign ally. The war of 1812 was fought and won by America alone.

- There was universal rejoicing in America at the end of the war, and most Americans considered the war to have been a successful victory. In Britain, there was a state of near mourning and a very strong sense that the government had sued for peace too soon and given up too much.

- Both surviving ex presidents (Adams and Jefferson) praised Madison for his conduct of the war, even though they were from opposite parties with very different ideas.

- In spite of the fact that the New England states defiantly failed to support the war and even kept trading with the enemy (Britain), there was no loss of civil liberties or freedoms of such anti-war radicals. Contrast this with the loyalists in the Revolutionary War who lost most of their property and were forced to flee the country; with the Japanese American citizens in World War II that were interred in prison camps for the duration of the war; with the loss of property and rights during the Civil War of southern supporters in the north, and northern supporters in the south; and with the anti-communist witch hunt that took place during the Korean war.

- While much undue attention has been laid on the burning of Washington by the British, it is too often overlooked that the US was more successful in taking the battle to the territory of the enemy than the other way around. The US campaign in Canada was successful in the end, in spite of some blundering US generals. And unlike the revolutionary war in which the British seized and held New York City for the duration, British attacks on the US were brief and not lasting, and gained no real territory for the enemy. Indeed, the British high-tailed it out of Washington as soon as they took it, since they knew they could not hold it.

- The US emerged from the war largely in control of the Great Lakes which previously had been controlled by the British, and also in control of the vital port of New Orleans, and having won an amazing number of naval battles against the strongest navy on earth.

And now to the details, many of which are surprising. The reason for the surprise is that Madison was so soundly criticized from all sides, and made so little effort to refute the mountain of falsehoods thrown at him, that many historians have been misled by the plethora of false documents of the times. In other words, many historians have believed some of the garbage and falsehoods that were constantly being thrown at Madison, and have repeated it in what they have written about him, wrongly assuming it to be true. In so doing they have demonstrated not Madison's weakness but their own--of being lazy and unwilling to dig and find the true story as a historian should! As Madison himself said, the story of the War of 1812 needs to be summarized by historians who penetrate below the surface of events and "beyond the horizon of unexpanded minds."[38]

And quite a story it was. Contrary to numerous false claims that Madison was ultimately bullied into declaring war by Congress, he in fact took the lead in the path to war, often in the face of a reluctant Congress. Madison did this because he wisely and prophetically knew that a tough response to Britain was needed, and that nothing short of war was likely to achieve America's goals. It therefore should come as no surprise that as early as 1809, when Madison was barely a few months into the presidency, he indicated that if Britain retained its 'Orders in Council' which denied America the right to trade with France, war was inevitable. As stated by one of the few historians who did his research and discovered the truth, "in his first fortnight in office, the new President moved from defensive embargo to threat and promise (within constitutional limits) of a resort to military action."[39]

Of course, many other historians have schizophrenically faulted Madison for 'rushing into war,' rather than avoiding it like his predecessors. Again, such a view demonstrates blindness to reality. If Madison had been determined to rush into war, why did it take him three years to do it? After all, this is the 'War of 1812' we are talking about, not the 'War of 1809.' The reality is that Madison gave Britain and France chance after chance after chance to avoid war. France finally got the message and started to change its policies. Britain got the message only after it was too late.

Perhaps putting the situation in modern terms might help. Suppose a nation today (call them "Nation A") seized American merchant ships at will on the high seas and kidnapped American sailors. How long would anyone expect the United States to hold back from swift and decisive military action against Nation A? And suppose another nation (call them "Nation B") seized American ships merely because they unloaded their cargo in the port of a country that Nation B did not like. Would the United States hold back from war if Nation B refused to change such a policy and kept seizing ship after ship? As Madison himself noted in 1809, there are circumstances such as these "leaving no choice but between absolute disgrace and resistance by force."[40]

In light of these examples, Madison's patience in the face of such outright belligerent acts of Great Britain and France is apparent. For three long years, Madison patiently prompted, scolded, urged and wrangled with these two countries about their policies. For three long years he put up with their endless excuses and flimsy justifications for acts that were clearly acts of war. For three long years Madison endured the ceaseless criticisms of the war hawks in Congress and the country who wanted action NOW, rather than more patient waiting. But in the end, unlike his illustrious predecessors, Madison never flinched from the ultimate fall-back position of armed conflict. This was no attorney afraid to go to trial, who could not reach a settlement because everyone knew he was afraid of facing a jury in the courtroom. This was no weak-kneed quarterback who was afraid to call the tough plays out of fear of criticism, or concern about taking risks. This was a man firm in his resolve to go to war if necessary rather than back down. Madison demonstrated the same resolve that the modern American public demands of its president today if foreign powers thumb their noses at us. He was not afraid to go to war after all other reasonable alternatives were attempted. And he did just that. But he didn't do it until all reasonable alternatives had been exhausted.

A review of the history of this era reveals a fascinating reality--Madison prophetically knew all along he was headed for war. This was no neophyte who insanely believed peace could be achieved if he tried hard and long enough. He was a realist who knew all along that war was almost certainly coming, and could only be averted by a miracle. Thus, it comes as no surprise that Madison in his first annual message to Congress in November 1809 strongly urged that military spending be increased so that the military could be prepared for "eventual situations" that were likely to evolve. In an act of supreme idiocy, Congress voted to decrease military spending instead. As subsequent events proved, Congress clearly lacked Madison's visionary and prophetic talents. What it didn't lack was the ability to later criticize Madison for failing to build up the military.

Of course, there are those who like to flip flop and once again criticize Madison for being too patient. Why did it take him three years to go to war? Why wait so long? The answer relates to more than just giving Britain and France a chance to repent and change their ways. Indeed, the answer is obvious to anyone who is familiar with war presidents and what they are faced with. It was the same problem faced by Woodrow Wilson between 1914-1917 prior to U.S. entry into World War I, by Franklin Roosevelt from 1939 to late 1941 prior to U.S. entry into World War II, and by Lyndon Johnson in the 1960s prior to and after U.S. entry into the Vietnam Conflict. As President Johnson learned to his chagrin, taking the country to war is not a good idea until the country is willing to go there. If you jump into conflict before enough people are willing to support it, you literally doom any such war to failure. Wars are not won by a public who does not believe in their cause. In short, it was not 'Mr. Madison's War' that was at issue, but the war of the people of America. As one historian noted, "to stir either nation [Britain or France] to a repeal of illegal edicts, the national spirit must be stimulated in the American people and transmitted to Congress." Or to put it in the blunter terms used by James Monroe to the French minister in 1810, "You know sir, that this government is based on public opinion."[41] It took Madison three years of prodding the American people before they were willing to do what he wanted to do in 1809.

After decreasing military spending, Congress in May of 1810 passed what was known as 'Macon Bill No. 2,' which in true Congressional tradition was an artful dodge of responsibility. This bill stated that all trade with Britain and France would be unrestricted. This meant that, in spite of the depredations of both the British and French in seizing ships which they believed had traded with their enemy, all British and French trading ships would be welcome in American ports. But if either nation rescinded their ridiculous laws directed at harming American shipping, American blockage of trade with the other nation would be restored three months later. Madison was disgusted, since he knew the result of this law would favor England which had the stronger navy. This was because British warships would keep most French trading ships from reaching American shores, while British ships would have free and unrestricted trade. Under such circumstances, Britain would obviously never rescind its 'Orders in Council' and cease impressing and kidnapping American sailors on the high seas.

The wily Napoleon rose to the bait. He instructed his minister to the United States to communicate that France would rescind its restrictive trade laws--even though he had no intention of doing so. Upon hearing the news Madison was guarded. Some foolish historians who once again failed to do their research have asserted that Madison was outfoxed and deceived by Napoleon. However, the record indicates that Madison knew Napoleon thought he was duping him, but Madison went along with it anyway because he also knew this would increase pressure on England which is where the real problem lay. Word was therefore sent to the British that restrictions on British trade would be restored in three months unless their 'Orders in Council' were rescinded. Naturally this did not occur, and so after three months British ships were once more blocked from American ports.

Madison was not surprised when Britain responded to this new blockage by demanding not only an end to the blockade of British ships, but that the Americans somehow do the impossible and stop the French from harming British trade. Such a demand was about as realistic as expecting a mouse to force a tomcat to behave. No wonder Madison was so firmly convinced that Britain's policy went beyond merely annoying France and restricting its trade, but was secretly aimed at completely undermining American independence and commercial growth. Indeed, he knew that the British desired to destroy the commercial prosperity of the United States because the US was becoming a manufacturing rival of Britain, particularly in the fledgling textile industry.

Meanwhile vilifications of Madison in the press continued unabated. Based on the ludicrous observation of a postmaster who had seen 12 letters pass between Madison and Jefferson between April and June, 1810, the report widely circulated that Madison was being controlled by the former president. In reality the letters contained no foreign policy discussions at all, but just talked about imported sheep and other meaningless matters. Indeed, poor Jefferson was so much in the dark about foreign policy he had to learn what was going on from newspapers. But such realities did not keep false charges from being leveled at Madison-- charges which he simply ignored. Sometimes the accusations bordered on the ridiculous. For example, the same edition of a Federalist newspaper accused Madison of both being (1) too weak to act in foreign affairs, and of (2) drawing a sword against the world's strongest military power. Clearly the Federalists could not have it both ways!

At this critical time, Madison found himself in need of a new Secretary of State to replace the marginally competent Robert Smith. He turned to an old friend and ally, James Monroe. The record once more casts light on reality and debunks one of the myths created by detractors and perpetuated by some lazy historians, that a spineless Madison was supposedly goaded into war by his Secretary of State Monroe. In reality, Monroe nearly declined the appointment because he thought Madison was getting to close to war![42]

It is not surprising that in the midst of the war on words and the constant barrage being leveled at the President that the new French Minister, Louis Serrurier, before he met Madison was duped into believing the President was a spineless jellyfish. Serrurier quickly changed his mind upon actually meeting the president and discovering his true nature. His conclusion after this meeting was that "Mr. Madison governs by himself ... [he had] more intelligence and knowledge of affairs than his secretaries ... [and was] not without some toughness of character when he thinks the national honor is involved." On another occasion Serrurier stated bluntly "The Secretaries of State, of the Treasury, and of War are undecided, perhaps, and act more according to events; but happily the President, superior to them in enlightenment as in position, governs entirely by himself."[43]

In the midst of this chaos of being caught in the crossfire between Britain and France, not to mention the crossfire between outraged

Federalists and unsupportive Republican members of his own party, Madison suddenly found himself dealing with the possibility of acquiring Florida as a new U.S. possession. Many both within and without the administration urged him to take action when it became known that dissidents in Florida were hoping for U.S. assistance in their effort to revolt from Spain, with the idea that the U.S. would then take them in as a new territory. Madison's policy was once again prophetic and sound. He refused to foment the disturbance or officially support it, but let it be known that if the dissidents were successful on their own and created an independent Florida, such territory would be welcomed under the United States umbrella. In short, he refused to take the bait and send in troops to attack Spain. And Madison was true to his word. When a revolt occurred in 'West Florida' (which today is the southernmost parts of Alabama and Georgia) and the area became free and independent, he quickly incorporated the new territory into the United States by executive action. But the bulk of Florida remained under Spanish control. His goal was to "merely hold what had been gained without bloodshed."[44]

By 1812, Madison was convinced that war was coming very soon. He again called on Congress to increase military spending. His

Secretary of the Treasury Albert Gallatin feared that the President's vocal support for war would be unpopular and result in his losing re-election, after which a new president would take office who would yield to appeasement and a "disgraceful peace." From this we see the debunking of yet another favorite theory of Madison's detractors and some lazy historians-- that Madison sought war in order to increase his chances for re-election. The truth was the opposite, as Madison continued consistently with the stand he had taken from the beginning, and hoped that voters would stand by him. At this time, Dolly Madison wrote confidentially to her sister, "I believe there will be war. Mr. Madison sees no end to the perplexities without it." As one historian who did his research noted, "The record as revealed in the British, French, and American archives, the papers of Madison, and the words of militant members of Congress, totally refutes the historical picture of the President as a passive observer or helpless opponent of congressional policies ... Desiring peace but believing war to be inevitable, he guided Congress toward that event and stimulated preparation for it."[45]

Federalists in Congress finally started to see the writing on the wall, so when Madison proposed raising an army of 10,000 men they did not oppose it too strongly. Rather, they supported an increase in the number to 35,000. However, their motive for this seeming shift was anything but supportive of Madison or the war. Rather, they knew that obtaining that many men would either be impossible or would greatly increase taxes, either of which would hurt the president. As Madison wryly observed, "They have provided, after two months delay, for a regular force requiring twelve [months] to raise it, and after three months for a volunteer force, on terms not likely to raise it at all."[46] As if this action by Congress wasn't bad enough, the legislators tossed out Madison's request to improve the navy by building 12 badly needed gunships of the line and 10 frigates. Instead, Congress decreased the allocation of funds to repair the frigates already in existence. The hope of Madison's detractors of course was that the embarrassment of an inadequate military would result in more blame being heaped on the President.

Some historians have faulted Madison for hesitancy or wishy-washiness in taking a seemingly long time to submit a war message to Congress. As noted above, if these historians had consulted the record they would have seen the reason--Madison felt that war should be declared by a large and influential majority in order to be sustainable. He held off presenting his message because he wanted to make sure there was enough support in the populace and in Congress to sustain a conflict. He personally had been ready for years for a declaration of war which he saw as inevitable as early as 1809, but had held off in order for public and congressional support for war to catch up to him. Interestingly, Federalists in Congress somehow convinced the British minister to the U.S., Augustus Foster, that Madison would never declare war but was merely blustering but never taking action in order to get both pro-war and anti-war supporters on his side so he could win the presidential election. Foster passed this nonsense on to Britain in his official communications, which unfortunately was largely believed there. Foster's surprise was truly great when he finally realized he had been deceived by the Federalists, and the United States was going to war.

As war commenced, it was suggested to Madison that laws be passed to punish those who did not support the war effort. This was particularly pertinent, since the New England states did not support the war, and indeed State officials looked the other way as their private merchants continued to trade with the enemy in direct violation of federal law. While Madison favored enforcement of federal law, he did not favor laws that limited free speech similar to the 'Alien and Sedition Acts' enacted by Congress during the Adams administration, which criminalized criticism of the administration. Obviously, such laws would be considerably more justified in 1812 than in Adams' day. Notwithstanding this, Madison refused to support such laws and on the contrary did all he could to prevent them, thereby leaving himself open to ongoing criticism. He had a "determination to maintain complete civil liberty in a passion-torn country rife with disloyalty. He held to that course throughout the war, in spite of slanders directed against himself unparalleled in American History." Indeed, "suppression of free speech in Madison's opinion was more damaging than the license it engendered."[47]

Madison tried to put pressure on Congress to do its duty and fund the war effort. However, he never used his power to issue 'executive orders' or attempted to usurp his way into the legislative field as so many of his war-president successors have done. Indeed, his behavior was in perfect accord with the War Powers Resolution passed by Congress 160 years later in 1973, which was enacted to prevent future presidents from committing troops to a Vietnam-style conflict without congressional approval. Madison steadfastly refused to engage in war without the consent of Congress. He left the decision for war in the hands of Congress because it is "a solemn question which the

Constitution wisely confides to the legislative department."[48] Once again, Madison's example as the first war president was fully in accord with the constitution, and it would have been a great benefit to the country if it had been followed by his successors.

As war commenced, just like Lincoln 40 years later, Madison was plagued by incompetent generals who failed to take command. His hope for a quick thrust into Canada to bring a swift request for peace from the British--truly a brilliant strategy--was ruined by timid generals who were afraid to act. Indeed, General Hull violated direct orders and surrendered his entire force of 2,500 men at Detroit without a fight, even though it was obvious to everyone (except him, apparently) that if he had fought he would have won. It is no more appropriate to blame Madison for the spinelessness of his generals than it would be to blame Lincoln for the same thing 4 decades later. Fortunately however, the war news was not all bad. The country was blessed with stout hearted naval officers who embarrassed the British beyond measure. Indeed, the war of 1812 is known for its many American naval victories both on the Great Lakes and the Atlantic, even though America started the war with a mere 14 warships pitted against more than 700 warships in the British fleet! Much of the American's success can be attributed to the fact that they always fired their canon at the waterline, puncturing hulls and sinking ships. The vain British Navy aimed its canons at masts and rigging in an attempt to make flight from battle impossible. Obviously if both sides had good canon aim in a fight, the British would be able to watch their foe rendered immobile, as they sank ingloriously beneath the waves to a watery grave.

Madison won the election of 1812 by a narrow margin. Indeed, he received only 50.4% of the popular vote, which was the closest margin of any presidential election to that time. In light of the war and the unparalleled negative press that constantly battered him, as well as the near treasonous revolt of the New England states from supporting the war or even complying with federal law, "the marvel was that he won at all."[49] The reason was that, much as Madison's enemies hated to admit it, no one as strong and capable as him was running against him. John Adams and Rufus King, both avowed Federalists, supported Madison over their own party nominee, DeWitt Clinton of New York.

As the war progressed, Madison's prophetic vision did not fail him. On May 24, 1814, fully three months before catastrophe struck, he foresaw the likelihood of an attack on the nation's capital. He immediately instructed his Secretary of War, John Armstrong, to prepare for it. Armstrong promised he would-- then did nothing. Part of Armstrong's justification for his inaction was that only Madison seemed to believe an attack on the nation's capital would happen. William Jones, Secretary of the Navy considered the idea as crazy, and so did James Monroe, Secretary of State. Notwithstanding their disbelief, Madison continued to insist that such an attack was likely and pushed Armstrong to make the necessary preparations. Armstrong just as consistently promised to get right to it--then did nothing. Frustrated, Madison finally created a military district in Maryland with General Winder appointed as commander. Unfortunately however, General Winder proved as incompetent as Armstrong and Hull.

One of the favorite activities of historians is to use the benefit of hindsight to point out things a President should have done that would have been better than what he did. The reason historians are not as famous as Presidents is that their gift of perceiving the proper course of action completely fails them when confronted with present problems, rather than having the benefit of hindsight. And so it is with Madison. He is continually faulted on all sides for almost everything he did. One of the favorite criticisms is that he should have fired Armstrong and Winder and Hull and other incompetents sooner than he did. No matter that Lincoln was also slow to fire similar incompetents in his day. Madison is therefore faulted for one of his greatest strengths, and for a virtue that is admired in Lincoln to this day--his compassion and willingness to give a guy a second chance. In the end, Armstrong and Winder both failed their second chance, and Madison asked them to resign.

Another false accusation raised against Madison is that he supposedly fled the capital when it was attacked in August, 1814. Nothing could be further from the truth. Rather than high-tailing it out of town, Madison hopped on a horse and headed for the sound of gunfire. Indeed, he is the only President in history to ride directly into a battle zone while President, completely oblivious to his own danger. He and Monroe took personal charge of military forces as both Armstrong and Windsor had proved incapable of doing so. As any historian who consults the facts will realize, if Madison had truly fled from the capital as alleged, the city would have given itself to the enemy since the citizens were on the verge of sending out a man with a white flag when Madison stopped them.[50] As it was, the British fled the city in haste, fearful of being surrounded and routed.

In the months that followed, the attack on Washington was viewed in all of Europe as a horrible British blunder, since it highlighted Britain's true policy--which Madison had known all along--that Britain's greatest goal was merely to humiliate America. The reality is, although Washington was burned, no military advantage was gained at all. It was an act intended to humiliate, and nothing more. This is why Madison believed the attack would come while no one else did--because he had a much better perception of British motives. It was simply not the same situation as the Revolutionary War in which New York (arguably the nation's capital in that day, in the minds of some) was taken and held by the British for the duration of the war. Everyone knew they could not have pulled off such a stunt in respect to Washington DC.

In spite of the obvious, crying need for an increase in the military, Congress continued throughout the war to hinder the President at every turn. The same was often true of military commanders responsible for prosecution of the war. An example is seen in Madison's struggle to get funding and support to increase the number of warships on the Great Lakes. Some of America's greatest victories had already occurred on the lakes, so naturally one would think there would be support for a build-up of American warships there. Not so. Madison had to fight, cajole and personally intervene for almost every ship. Being gifted with prophetic vision as he was, he knew that America's domination of the Great Lakes was essential not only during the war but for the decades that would follow it. Otherwise Great Britain with its vaunted navy would dominate the region and the surrounding land, inhibiting growth and territorial expansion. Once again, Madison's prophetic vision carried the day, and the necessary ships were finally funded. And forever after, the Great Lakes were known as largely American territory.

And then there was New Orleans. It was commonly believed that whoever controlled New Orleans would likewise control expansion in the west, since shipping down the Mississippi River had no alternative but to pass out of New Orleans into the Gulf of Mexico. Not surprisingly therefore, the British sent a large contingent of troops down to the area, and Madison sent Andrew Jackson and a hefty mass of troops to provide a defense. By now (1814), the war was supposed to be over and everyone knew it. But stubborn as usual, the British were unwilling to yield until they had plucked this one last ripe fruit--which would enable them to continue to harass and humiliate the fledgling United States for decades by preventing the new nation's westward expansion. Madison was just as stubborn, and in a way was almost grateful the

British were forcing the issue. Best to settle once and for all just who would dominate in the west. He once again prophetically said, "'If the English force us to continue the war, they will make us do in ten years [take control of the west] what we perhaps would not do in half a century."[51] And once again, he was dead right.

But that wasn't fully known at the time. Federalists gloatingly predicted that New Orleans would fall, and the humiliation and U.S. weakness this would demonstrate would both force Madison to resign in embarrassment and for the nation to call on New England to save the union. Indeed, some were calling for Madison's impeachment at this time. The treasonous 'Hartford Convention' of New England met at the same time as the troops lined up in New Orleans. The convention met in secret. Although they were not planning to secede, they were craftily forming plans about how to take control of the government once Madison resigned. It was common knowledge that if New England had not been so flagrantly against the war from the beginning, the British would have sued for peace far sooner. The British goal of demoralizing the new nation seemed assured if they could divide the people, and so they kept trying to divide them.

Madison again had all the justification and incentive in the world to take action against the traitors--and steadfastly refused. The long-term harm that would result from violating New England's freedom of speech was not justified in his prophetic mind by a short-term gain. Benjamin Lear noted that this "second war of independence" occurred without any trials for treason or slander, which was truly amazing. Speaking of Madison he said, "His name will descend to posterity with that of our illustrious Washington. One achieved our independence, and the other sustained it." Indeed, one historian noted that "his refusal to abridge freedom of speech and press saved the country from civil war." But not everyone was as visionary or pleased with Madison's restraint. "Madison's refusal to employ force or vigilante methods against New England brought cries of despair" from those who thought detractors of the war should be punished.[52]

The reality is, Madison seemed to be practically the only one to keep his head during the intense war of words and bullets that raged all around him. French Minister Serrurier saw the President's resilient firmness as the chief reason the nation had the ability to keep on fighting. Serrurier marveled "that a government so badly armed should be able to fight alone, and with success" against powerful England, "with so active a hostile faction at the heart of the nation." One historian noted that "he held the nation to its course with unfaltering determination in the face of military adversities and New England sedition," and further that the "consensus of opinion [was] that the Madison administration had set the country on the road to internal development, national strength and economic independence, without weakening the fabric of self-government. That was the legacy of the War of 1812."[53]

Jackson routed the British at New Orleans, even though the battle technically took place after peace had been declared. But due to the slowness of communication, Jackson fortunately did not know this. With the gain of New Orleans, the west was guaranteed to the United States. Britain was disgraced instead of disgracing America, and the war ended on a high note. The representative from the Hartford Convention arrived in Washington in a classic case of bad timing--just as news of the New Orleans victory reached the city. He quickly left in embarrassment. Indeed, so great was the embarrassment of the Federalists that their entire party collapsed and soon ceased to exist. Suddenly and rather unexpectedly, Madison was hailed as a hero.

So was the war really a draw as many historians have subsequently claimed? Hardly. The general mood in America and Britain tell the tale--while there was rejoicing in America, mourning and embarrassment prevailed in England. Many in the mother country felt their government had given up the fight at the worst possible moment, and had nothing to show for years of conflict. As French Minister Serrurier said, "all is loss for England; all is gain for the United States ... Finally the war has given the Americans what they so essentially lacked, a national character founded on a glory common to all." As one historian noted, "the war had produced an expansion of manufactures that could not have been achieved in twenty years of peace. It had proved the Union to be indissoluble ... Three years of trial had proved the capacity of republican institutions to sustain a state of war."[54] Madison with his usual gift of vision characterized the Revolutionary War as a struggle in America's infancy, while the War of 1812 was a successful conflict in its much stronger youth.[55]

At this heady moment, some called on a re-allocation of the troops in New Orleans, to march forth and liberate Texas. Madison refused, viewing such an action as being extra-legal and illegitimate. He stated, "a respect for authority of the laws alone obliges the Executive to prevent these enterprises."[56] Madison had a great respect for the sovereignty of nations. This included the unique "nations" within the United States, consisting of the Indian tribes. In 1815 he sent troops to kick invading whites off Indian lands in the south, and negotiated a road across Indian land on their own terms.

Madison also illustrated how to handle an arms buildup--a phenomenon common in modern times. After the war was over, it became known that the British intended to build up their presence of warships on the Great Lakes. Madison quickly responded with a show of both strength and diplomacy. He first ordered that U.S. warships planned or under construction for use on the lakes were to be quickly completed. But at the same time he directed John Quincy Adams, U.S. ambassador to England, to negotiate for a reduction of arms on the lakes. This two-pronged approach protected the nation no matter what happened, but promoted a peaceful resolution.

Madison was the first and arguably the greatest war president. His example of consistent, steadfast pressure towards his foreign policy goals was closely linked to an undeviating allegiance to the constitution. No matter what the cost, Madison would not violate constitutional principles, even if doing so would presumably help the war effort. He never let short-term gains of the moment overcome long term principles. If succeeding presidents had but followed his example, the history of America's foreign policy would be a far more honorable and pleasant story to read.

NOTES:

[37] Brandt, at 499.

[38] 8 Hunt at 407 (1908).

[39] Brandt at 411.

[40] 8 Hunt, at 86.

[41] Brandt, at 431, 464.

[42] Ibid at 455.

[43] Ibid at 460-461, 464.

[44] Ibid at 463.

[45] Ibid at 472-475.

[46] 8 Hunt, at 176.

[47] Brandt, at 504, 547.

[48] 8 Hunt, at 200.

[49] Brandt, at 526.

[50] Ibid at 576.

[51] Ibid at 581.

[52] Ibid at 583, 590, 599.

[53] Ibid at 582, 590, 598.

[54] Ibid at 589.

[55] 8 Hunt, at 407.

[56] Brandt, at 594.

CHAPTER SIX
All About Money

Historians tend to view Alexander Hamilton as the primary financial genius among the founding fathers, and probably with good reason. His policies enabled the fledgling and nearly bankrupt new country to achieve rapid prosperity and growth. Few today question that Hamilton was able to accomplish the nearly impossible task of bringing financial stability to what previously was near chaos. Such is his legacy.

But that does not mean his road to financial health was the only one that could have been trod. Jefferson and Madison opposed many of Hamilton's financial policies not out of a dimsighted failure to perceive financial realities, but because they firmly believed there were other methods that could achieve similar success without compromising, as they saw it, the hard-fought principles of government in the new constitution. In short, Madison was no financial neophyte who lacked understanding. In finances, as in most matters, he was once again a genius. As such, he saw fundamental problems that would result from unsound financial practices--the very practices that we see so rampantly around us in America today.

For Madison, the government's financial matters were to be addressed pursuant to simple, fundamental principles such as frugality, honesty and avoidance of extravagance. Indeed, in April of 1787 he stated succinctly "it is too often forgotten, by nations as well as by individuals, that honesty is the best policy."[57]

Yct hc was no miser either, since as we saw in the previous chapter he strongly advocated defense spending when most in Congress thought it unimportant. He additionally believed that strict enforcement of debts--which was usually motivated by greed-- should be tempered by morality and humanity. In short, Madison saw money as a tool, rather than an end in itself. Strict laws applicable to how this tool worked should usually be followed, but not at the expense of the people the tool was meant to serve.

A few examples will illustrate Madison's financial views. In 1788, Madison clearly favored free trade with minimal government interference--a point of view obviously more aligned with the thinking of the modern Republican party than the Democratic party he and Jefferson are commonly assumed to have created. He doubted that government had the wisdom to supersede or properly control the free market. Said Madison:

"I own myself the friend to a very free system of commerce, and hold it as a truth, that commercial shackles are generally unjust, oppressive, and impolitic; it is also a truth, that if industry and labor are left to take their own course, they will generally be directed to those objects which are the most productive, and this in a more certain and direct manner than the wisdom of the most enlightened legislature could point out ... thus all are benefitted by exchange, and the less this exchange is cramped by Government, the greater are the proportions of benefit to each."[58]

But Madison was wise enough to realize that there are exceptions to every rule, and that government involvement in the economy was sometimes necessary. The trick was to identify the dividing line between what was acceptable and what went too far. In this regard, Madison noted:

"If my general principal is a good one, that commerce ought to be free, and labor and industry left at large to find its proper object, the only thing which remains will be to discover the exceptions that do not come within the rule I have laid down ... this ought to be for the general good of society."[59]

Hence, Madison was the first to acknowledge that a completely free economy was not necessarily a good one. This concept is closer to the thinking of the modern Democratic Party than the Republicans. There are times and circumstances in which the economy must be directed by government action "for the general good of society." As he stated more succinctly on another occasion, "I am a friend to free commerce, and at the same time, a friend to such regulations as are calculated to promote our own interest, and this on national principles."[60]

So what exceptions did Madison see to a governmental 'hands-off' policy regarding the economy? He named several. First on his list, which were a big issue in his day, were duties (tariffs) on imports brought by foreign vessels. Madison noted that if Americans did not create such duties they would be injuring themselves, since other countries would not reciprocate and allow free trade in their ports by American merchant ships. Hence, he believed that a government tariff policy favoring American manufactured goods was well founded for the betterment of the people. In short, he had an 'America first' policy, similar to many today.

Madison recognized however that import duties could have a negative side affect on American manufacturing. Raw goods needed in the manufacturing process which came from abroad would only be attainable at a higher after-tariff price. This could limit and damage American manufacturing. For this reason he stated "there may be some manufactures which ... can advance toward perfection without any adventitious [government] aid, while others, for want of the fostering hand of government, will be unable to go on at all."[61] Hence, government intervention in the economy for the encouragement of manufacturing was among his list of exceptions. This was an enlightening exception for a person in his day, and acknowledged the need for government involvement in some economic matters.

In respect to other exceptions where government interference in the economy was justified, he noted the obvious exceptions of defense spending and financial action against enemies in times of war. He did not feel the same however about "sumptuary prohibitions"-- government regulations intended to alter or re-direct general consumer spending. He felt the government should not get involved in such matters since, as he said "I do not, in general, think any great national advantage arises from restrictions passed on this head."[62] This was because commodities on the open market had in his view "a distinction in point of value"-- in other words, their value, or price, varied depending on unrestricted supply and demand. For Madison, there was no national advantage in governmental meddling with the demand, supply or price of such commodities.

As noted above, one of the chief sources of governmental revenue in Madison's day were import duties, or tariffs. Madison noted that such tariffs could be enacted "without injury to the community," and that they had the double benefit of protecting "domestic manufactures" and also of raising revenue. Most importantly however, Madison believed tariffs on trade were a good way of raising revenue for the government because it was "preferable to laying a general tax." Hence, Madison was not fond of a general tax to be laid directly on the populace. Such taxes would reduce the spending capabilities of the common man, and were especially dangerous if they were "perpetual," or in other words ongoing taxes as compared to one-time tax events. He said: "To pass a [tax] bill not limited in duration, which was to draw revenue from the pockets of the people appeared to be dangerous in the administration of any government ... He imagined it might be considered by their constituents as incompatible with the spirit of the Constitution, and dangerous to republican principles."[63]

Such comments may seem extreme to us today, accustomed as we are to the yearly mad rush of income tax filing each April 15th. The idea of a non-perpetual income tax is completely foreign to us. How could the government go on without a perpetual income tax? Once again Madison prophetically foresaw this 'expectation of and dependency on endless taxes' mentality, and that is why he warned so strongly against the initial creation of perpetual taxes. He disliked any tax which was not tied to a specific purpose, and which focused instead on raising "the revenue itself which without any appropriation might continue flowing into the public treasury independent of the will of the people, and might thereby become a convenience in the hands of some other department of the government, for the purpose of oppression." The better way was to earmark taxes for specific purposes and limit their duration, since "If the [tax] bill was to be made perpetual, it would be continued after the purpose for which it was adopted was ceased; the error would in this case be irremediable; whereas if its limitation was determined it would always be in the power of the Government to make it commensurate with what the public debts and contingencies required."[64]

Madison acknowledged that direct taxation of the people "will not be applied to until it is found that sufficient funds cannot be obtained in any other way."[65] Hence, he did not shoot down all direct taxes. However, he noted that setting up a system of perpetual taxation would create an endless need for ever increasing tax assessments. Under this mode of thinking, government agencies will develop the idea that their funding is a right rather than a privilege, and will always come up with ways to justify and spend their allotment of tax dollars. If each direct tax of the people was limited in duration and targeted for a specific purpose, government agencies would be forced to trade their 'perpetual duration' mindset for one of accountability and frugality. This in turn would revolutionize the way government budgets are handled in the United States.

It is easy for us to assume that this must be one of the exceptions to Madison's genius, and that things have changed so much that his financial advice cannot realistically be applied to us today. However, just because Madison's comments seem foreign to our experience, that does not mean he is wrong. Indeed, if we remove ourselves from the 'perpetual tax' mode of thinking, we begin to see that we are more likely to be the ones with skewed thinking, rather than Madison. Just imagine if Congress today had to tie every tax it passed to a specific purpose and put a deadline on when it would end! Imagine how much better citizens would feel actually knowing what their tax dollars are going to be spent for. Imagine how much less the tax burden would be if government administrators did not have an always-certain allotment of funds coming their way, but had to justify every penny, just like in private business. Imagine the different world we would live in if this simple and prophetic insight from James Madison were adopted and followed today.

For Madison, no direct tax should endure beyond two years. The reason was simple: two years was the term of office of members of the House of Representatives, who had the constitutional mandate to originate all money bills. Any tax longer than this would pass out of their control, which was contrary to the intent of the founders. He said:

"The Constitution as had already been observed, places the power in the House of originating money bills. The principal reason why the Constitution had made this distinction was, because they were chosen by the people and supposed to be best acquainted with their interests and ability. In order to make them more particularly acquainted with these objects, the democratic branch of the legislature consisted of a greater number, and were chosen for a shorter period, so that they might revert more frequently to the mass of the people. Now, if a revenue law was made perpetual, however unequal its operation might be it would be out of the power of this house to effect an alteration."[66]

Closely related to the issue of taxation is that of deficit spending, or in other words spending tomorrow's money today. The U.S. has continuously engaged in deficit spending since the 1930s, and it is currently considered standard policy to do so. Madison strongly disagreed with this idea, and decried "the practice by each generation of taxing the principal of its debts on future generations."[67] He further stated that he had "never been a proselyte to the doctrine that public debts are public benefits. I consider them, on the contrary, as evils which ought to be removed as fast as honor and justice will permit, and shall heartily join in the means necessary for that purpose."[68] And on another occasion he stated bluntly, "I go on the principle that a public debt is a public curse, and in a representative government a greater [curse] than in any other." One of the reasons was that "In order to relieve public credit sinking under the weight of an enormous debt, we invent new expenditures."[69] Once again, Madison was prophetic. He saw the vicious cycle of ever increasing debt and expenditure that occurs under deficit spending, like a dog endlessly chasing its tail.

Some may think Madison's views too stodgy and old fashioned for today's world, and may assert that advice of freeing the economy from government control and eliminating perpetual taxes would injure the downtrodden members of society who turn to government for support. However, any view of Madison as a dispassionate ogre would be grossly inaccurate. An example of this is seen in his views toward redeeming the 'continental' notes and IOUs that had circulated as currency during the revolutionary war.

In the early 1790s a debate emerged over whether current holders of 'continentals' and IOUs should be paid the face value of their notes. These 'continentals' and IOUs were issued by the Continental Congress during and immediately after the Revolutionary War in order to fund the war effort. The notes were the principal method of paying the soldiers, but since they were not immediately redeemable and depended entirely on the faith of the people in the Continental Congress and payment at an unknown future day, they depreciated rapidly. In short, people who received them could not cash them and did not think they were worth much. In order to not take a total loss on them, many holders of 'continentals' and IOUs sold them to speculators at significant discounts, often at a mere 10% of their face value. Purchasers of such notes had a vague hope that the notes would be profitable someday.

Their hopes were unexpectedly realized when Alexander Hamilton, as part of his financial policy, proposed paying face value to all current holders of continentals and IOUs, as a way to increase confidence that the new government would follow through and pay its debts. Madison didn't necessarily oppose this, but was among those who felt that paying solely the current holders of the notes would be unfair, and that the original holders should get something as well. As such Madison refused to take the hard line of Hamilton and others who felt that strict enforcement of the notes according to their written terms, and only for the benefit of whoever currently held them, was the best policy. Madison preferred a more humanitarian policy that also recognized and paid for the significant sacrifices and contributions made by the original holders of the notes. For America to pay current holders of the continentals and IOUs while ignoring the persons who first received them would "erect the monuments of her [America's] gratitude, not to those who saved her liberties, but to those who had enriched themselves in her funds." Madison further expounded on the matter thus:

"[T]he claims of the original holders, not less than those of the actual holders, should be fairly examined and justly decided ... A debt was fairly contracted: according to justice and good faith it ought to have been paid in gold or silver; a piece of paper only was substituted. Was this paper equal in value to gold or silver? No. It was worth, in the market ... no more than one-eighth or one-seventh of that value. Was this depreciated paper freely accepted? No. The government offered that or nothing. The relation of the individual to the government, and the circumstances of the offer, rendered the acceptance a forced, not a free one ... There are even cases where ... the property of the planter or farmer had been taken at the point of the bayonet, and a certificate presented in the same manner. But why did the creditors part with their acknowledgement of the debt? In some instances, from necessity, in others from a well-founded distrust of the public [government]. Whether from the one or the other they had been injured, they had suffered loss through the default of the debtor; and the debtor cannot, in justice or honor, take advantage of the default."[70]

This does not sound like a man who is all about money, and cares little for the downtrodden. Indeed, it demonstrates the opposite. Madison cared about those who had fought and bled and died, but not been paid. He cared for the poor who had been used by the government and speculators. It was patently unfair and heartless to let their needs be ignored and let the speculators be enriched.

While Madison felt the original holders of the notes should be paid, he nevertheless recognized the importance of paying the speculators something as well. Hence, he recognized and agreed with Hamilton that public faith in the government would be enhanced by payments to current note holders. His main point of disagreement had to do with payment to the original holders too, which Hamilton did not want to do. Madison's position was obviously motivated by compassion rather than economic sense. Madison's solution was simple--pay both. He stated that payment should be made to creditors and "let it be a liberal one in favor of the present holders, let them have the highest price which has prevailed in the market; and let the residue belong to the original sufferers. This will not do perfect justice; but it will do more real justice, and perform more of the public faith, than any other expedient proposed."[71]

Madison's position was soundly criticized as being too generous. Such complaints sound familiar today, since many in our day believe that strict enforcement of monetary obligations is the best and only policy, and that financial mercy is unwise. Being the genius that he was, Madison saw both sides of the argument, but felt that humanity and forgiveness were more noble and cherished positions than hard-core enforcement. He noted that he "had been animadverted upon [criticized] for appealing to the heart as well as the head; he would be bold, nevertheless, to repeat that in great and unusual questions of morality, the heart is the best judge."[72]

The essence of Madison's thinking on financial matters was to be generous to those who deserved it, but strict to those who did not. This can be seen in his position regarding 'paper money,' which was considered to be a common evil in his day. All of the state governments during the Revolutionary War and afterward printed paper money as a way to pay their debts. They quickly learned that much of the debt itself would be wiped out because the paper money itself devalued so quickly. They also realized they could help their debtor citizens by passing laws forcing creditors to accept payment of debts in paper money, which many states did. Hence, by way of example, if a man incurred a debt for $100, he could pay the full amount a year later with paper money that in reality was worth only around $20 by then. In those unstable times, since paper money devalued so rapidly it was nearly impossible for an adequate interest rate to be put on debts that would cover the loss created by devaluation of the paper currency. So pervasive was this evil of dodging legitimate debts that the constitutional convention of 1787 purposely inserted into Article 1, section 10 of the Constitution that "No State shall ... make any Thing but gold and silver Coin a Tender in Payment of Debts ..."

Madison spoke against the evil of paper money as a way to avoid debts on a number of occasions. This was not a situation where he felt financial mercy was appropriate. Rather, he felt that legitimate debts should be paid at their face value, barring an agreement to the contrary between the parties. On one occasion in speaking of the government's debt he said "The United States owe the value they received, which they acknowledge, and which they have promised to pay: what is that value? It is a certain sum in principal, bearing an interest of six percent. No logic, no magic, in my opinion, can diminish the force of the obligation."[73]

And then in speaking of paper money, he noted that "The antients [sic] were surely men of more candor than we are; they contended openly for an abolition of debts in so many words, while we strive as hard for the same thing under the ... specious pretense of a circulating medium ... for where is there a greater act of despotism than that of issuing paper money to depreciate for the purpose of paying debts, on easy terms?" On another occasion, Madison stated bluntly that paper money "affects rights of property as much as taking away equal value in land."[74]

In short, state use of paper money to avoid debt was an evil that Madison fought against with all his might. He saw a clear distinction between this and the payment of continentals, where compassion was warranted to avoid unfairness. Debtors who incurred an obligation should pay it, rather than expecting their state government to wipe it out for them. In short, there was a time for compassion and a time for strict enforcement, and the wisdom was in knowing the difference.

Finally, no discussion of Madison's views regarding money would be complete without discussing the national bank. In 1790 Alexander Hamilton proposed creation of a national bank as a way to help stabilize the finances of the fledgling country. Jefferson and Madison saw this proposal as a subtle way that rich merchants in the north could become richer at the expense of poor southern farmers. Much of the reason had to do with the distance from the bank. This was long before modern days of online banking, which has reduced the distance to the bank to total insignificance. In those days, advantages of a single central bank such as the one Hamilton wanted would mainly accrue to those near it, while citizens far away would gain little.

An example will illustrate. Bank notes given out by the bank could be redeemed or traded in for 'specie,' or in other words gold and silver coins. "But can any man say," said Madison, "that the bank notes will circulate at par in Georgia? ... we know that they cannot be made equal to specie, remote from the place where they can be immediately converted into coin; they must depreciate in case of a demand for specie." In other words, there was a transportation cost added to a bank note in Georgia that did not exist with a bank note in New York. Since the note could only be redeemed at the one and only bank up north, a distant note had less value because of this distance factor. And aggravating this problem even further was the reality noted by Madison-- with a reference to economic genius Adam Smith and his (then) recent book 'The Wealth of Nations'--that the existence of the bank and its notes would tend to increase the flow of bank notes in the economy, while gold and silver coins would flow less and would come to be held in the bank's vault. Hence, a note holder in Georgia would be truly stuck. Either he attempted to pay for items with his depreciated bank note or he resorted to using tobacco as money, since the bank had sucked most of the gold and silver out of the economy. These are not problems we face today, but are issues that truly existed in that day. Because of this, Madison noted that "the advantages [of a bank] would be better obtained by several banks, properly distributed, than by a single one."[75] But Hamilton's initial proposal was solely for a single bank, although branches in different locations were added later, after it was adopted. This helps explain why Madison so strongly opposed Hamilton's proposed bank, but later in 1816 supported a national bank that would have branches in the various states.

Another problem that Madison saw with a national bank was prophetic indeed. He noted that establishing a national bank could ultimately mean "exposing the public and individuals to all the evils of a run on the bank, which would be particularly calamitous in so great a country as this." Madison foresaw in 1790 what happened in the crash of 1929, in which 1/3 of the country's banks failed! He then noted that a run on the bank "might happen from various causes, as false rumors, bad management of the institution, an unfavorable balance of trade from short crops, &c."[76] It must be remembered that this was long before the Federal Reserve System and government guaranties of all bank funds. Banks in that day guarantied their own funds, with no government support. Putting too much faith in banks under these circumstances could be fatal, since any of a number of things could trigger a run on the bank. The economy is more than banks, and it should never be assumed that banks will somehow prevent economic distress. Banks are merely businesses that deal with a unique commodity--money. But like any business, they can be mismanaged or suffer other ills, and thereby spread panic and discouragement among the people.

Finally, Madison viewed a national bank as being not being supported by a constitutional provision. Not only was there no provision for incorporation of a national bank anywhere in the constitution, but as a former delegate to the constitutional convention Madison "well recollected that a power to grant charters of incorporation had been proposed in the General Convention and rejected."[77] He did not agree with Hamilton that the power of incorporating a bank could be implied from other constitutional provisions, such as the 'necessary and proper' clause.

Madison lost his battle to prevent Hamilton's bank. The First Bank of the United States was incorporated and began its life in 1791. It started out as just one bank, but later a few branch banks were added. The legislation creating the bank gave it a 20 year life, which at the time seemed rather lengthy. Ironically, at the end of that twenty year period Madison was president, and had the power to veto any bank bill enacted by the legislature. In point of fact, the bank lapsed in 1811 and ceased to exist for several years of Madison's presidency, amidst cries that it should be reinstated. By 1815, in light of the financial difficulties in America caused by the recent war with Great Britain, Madison was willing to support the bank instead of oppose it. He no longer opposed it as unconstitutional, noting rather that its existence for twenty years had legitimized it "by repeated recognitions under varied circumstances of the validity of such an institution in acts of the legislative, executive, and judicial branches of the government, accompanied by indications in different modes of a concurrence of the general will of the nation."[78] Hence, Madison indicated that a constitutional interpretation--even though somewhat dubious to begin with--could become constitutional by long-standing adoption and practice.

In early 1815 a new bank bill was enacted by Congress and came across Madison's desk. He vetoed it, but not because he was opposed to establishment of a national bank. Indeed, he was now guardedly in favor of such a bank even though this position was against the expressed wishes at the time of Thomas Jefferson and James Monroe. Rather, his veto was issued because this particular bill had been so watered down by the Senate (led by Calhoun) that the bank lacked the ability to loan badly needed money to the government. Something stronger was needed. Madison again vetoed a new bank bill a year later in January 1816, for similar reasons. It simply failed to allow the bank to do all it needed to do. Finally, on April 10, 1816, Madison signed into law a new bank bill passed by Congress. Thus a new national bank was born for another 20 years. It was destined to have a checkered history that terminated in the administration of Andrew Jackson, who was opposed to it.

Madison's views of banks is summed up by a statement he made in 1827 in which he noted that "they have taken too deep and wide a root in social transactions to be got rid of altogether, if that were desirable ... they have a hold on public opinion, which alone would make it expedient to aim rather at the improvement than the suppression of them."[79] In other words, a way needed to be found to live with banks, rather than drive them out of existence. But his views were not held by everyone.

What lessons can we learn from Madison's views on the national bank? First that any financial matter undertaken by the federal government needs to operate equally in favor of all the people in all parts of the country, to be fair. Second, that there is no evil in embracing a financial position formerly opposed if it is found to work well. Third, that governmental involvement in banking was legitimate, within constitutional bounds of course.

Finally, it must be noted that Madison practiced what he preached. He was not one to advocate financial accountability and frugality without following such principles in his private life. One of the best examples is seen when he traveled to Annapolis as President to inspect a new ship. Madison considered the trip as unofficial and insisted on paying his own fare rather than letting the government foot the bill.[80] Just imagine if presidents today did this!

James Madison saw our day. He saw our economic struggles and inconsistencies, and how burdened we have become with taxes. He saw government's need to avoid improper taxes, and the people's need to apply fundamental principles of thrift, integrity, simplicity and constitutional fidelity, tempered with compassion and new financial interpretations in those rare cases where such were justified. He was hesitant of banks, but was willing to live with them if they could be properly controlled. If we would but heed Madison's advice on frugality, budgeting, taxation and honesty, most of our financial woes of today would be greatly ameliorated.

NOTES:

[57] 2 Hunt, at 367 (1901).

[58] 5 Hunt, at 342.

[59] Id. at 343 (emphasis added).

[60] Id. at 349.

[61] Id at 344.

[62] Id.

[63] Id. at 345, 359.

[64] Id. at 360.

[65] Id. at 354 (emphasis added).

[66] Id. at 360.

[67] 6 Hunt, at 91.

[68] 5 Hunt, at 446.

[69] 6 Hunt at 11, 80.

[70] 5 Hunt at 448.

[71] Id. at 444.

[72] Id. at 449.

[73] Id. at 442.

[74] 2 Hunt at 280, 403.

[75] 6 Hunt at 26, 39.

[76] Id at 26.

[77] Id.

[78] 8 Hunt, at 327.

[79] 9 Hunt, at 282.

[80] Brandt at 598.

CHAPTER SEVEN
Nothing But Flowers in our Garden:
Madison's Views on Entertainment

Entertainment in the United States today is big business. Take television for instance. Reality show competitors secretly confide their hatred of their fellow competitors to the camera and therefore to the world, while millions of approving fans watch in delight. Pseudo-competitions of all kinds abound, including cake-making, modeling, losing weight, spending the least on home repairs and even having the "best" Christmas light display. House hunters are always given three choices of homes to choose from, and talk show hosts are always asking questions about sex since they apparently have nothing else on their minds.

And then there are the movies. The movie industry and what it produces is often taken more seriously by many than real life. The plots of major blockbusters are usually better known than one's neighbors; the personalities of fictional characters are often better understood and more discussed than one's own children or spouse. Meanwhile, movie stars make millions and spend their time off screen faking a desire to stay out of the lime light, while secretly making sure the tabloids are never too far away to photograph their profiles. And since the big bucks hinge on ratings, movie producers make sure their shows contain just the right amount of blood, gore, graphic sex, rudeness, profanity and brutality to get the 'right' rating.

Closely related is the music industry, where singers are worshiped as idols no matter how depraved their personal life-styles. Pop stars are born in a day, and even if they lose their TV competitions they come off as winners, since their faces have been plastered all over TV and the internet. Music is on constantly, no matter where one goes (except the library, of course). Many people are so addicted to their songs they must have them on in the shower, while they sleep, and during life-altering events such as final exams, weddings and funerals, and life-and-death hospital operations.

And then of course, there are sports. This make-believe world of endless championships, competitions, bowls, playoffs and series never ceases to generate interest. Never mind the illogic of grown men bashing themselves silly on the football field, or in baseball seeing how hard they can hit a ball with a stick. Of course, the ultimate ball and stick game is golf, where otherwise sane individuals are expected to smack a tiny ball hundreds of feet through the air, past intentionally planted traps and snares of all kinds, to land in a tiny gopher hole. Truly, if an alien were to visit modern America and see its sports contests, he would either choke from laughter at the insanity of it all, or leave the planet in disgust, sure that its inhabitants were nothing more than witless, game-absorbed freaks. Not that sports are bad in and of themselves. But they can be taken too far.

And what of the founders, such as James Madison? Would they view the insane, modern world of entertainment in the same way as an alien from another planet? And as for Madison himself, just what does this short little man, now long dead, have to contribute to modern America's obsession with endless entertainment? How can he enlighten us regarding the next blockbuster movie we should go see, the 'game of the century' that we just can't miss, or the TV series that is sure to be this season's hit?

Obviously he can't. But more than that, even if he were with us he wouldn't. What he has to say about entertainment is not likely to be popular. But it is a message that needs to be said, particularly in light of America's entertainment-obsession which produces failing schools and growing criminality.

From a young age Madison eschewed the pursuit of entertainment for its own sake as a waste of precious time. Recall from chapter two the words of Benjamin Rush about Madison's entertainment as a college student. It is worth repeating. Unlike the drinking, partying college student of today for whom education appears to be a secondary concern, Rush had this to say about Madison while at the same time advising his son to avoid worthless entertainment pursuits:

"I do not advise you against such exercises as are necessary to health, but simply to avoid sharing in what are commonly called 'plays.' The celebrated Mr. Madison when a student at the Jersey College never took part in them. His only relaxation from study consisted in walking and conversation. Such was the character he acquired while at college, that Dr. Witherspoon said of him to Mr. Jefferson (from whom I received the anecdote) that during the whole time he was under his tuition he never knew him to do nor to say an improper thing."[81]

Of course, some may disbelieve Rush and think that perhaps he and Dr. Witherspoon must have been joking. Surely no one could study that much and lead that boring of a life! Didn't Madison at least read one of the hot new fiction books coming off the press, like the ones in our day which generate large followings and midnight lines at bookstores on their release date?

Hardly. While Madison was an avid reader, he rarely wasted his time with fiction, which he termed 'books of fancy.' Listen to what Madison had to say about such writings in 1774 two years after he left Princeton. In a letter to his friend William Bradford, he said:

"I myself used to have too great a hankering after those amusing studies. Poetry, wit, and criticism, romances, plays, &c., captivated me much; but I began to discover that they deserve but a small portion of a mortal's time, and that something more substantial, more durable, and more profitable, befits a riper age. It would be exceedingly improper for a laboring man to have nothing but flowers in his garden, or to determine to eat nothing but sweet meats and confections. Equally absurd would it be for a scholar and a man of business to make up his whole library with books of fancy, and feed his mind with nothing but such luscious performances."[82]

For Madison, life was to be an ongoing conquest of the mind combined with service to the community, rather than an endless quest for entertainment that takes a person nowhere and produces nothing lasting. Each person has a duty to learn and discover new things in a never-ending pursuit of knowledge and excellence, and then to share what he has gained with others. Wasting one's mental powers and precious time on fanciful entertainments was a demonstration of folly, and showed a shallow mind, unwilling to engage in deeper thought.

Madison had no hesitation in applying the same standard to members of his immediate family. For example, in 1779 he commented on the education of his younger brother 'Willey.' After discussing various educational options, he recommended a private tutor, stating "I would recommend his being put under the instruction of Mr. Maury rather than suffer him to be idle at home."[83] Idleness was unthinkable, and idle pursuits of the young (which in our day are provided through game systems, the internet or cable TV) would have appalled him. Life was work and study and growth and learning and service. One can hardly read more than a few pages of his writings to see that he was constantly engaged in every facet of life around him, from politics to crop raising, and from the growth of nations to the management of farm animals. In short, he was just like his good friend Thomas Jefferson, who never ceased to study and learn and do new things, and then to share what he had gained with others.

Believe it or not however, in spite of all that has been said so far, Madison did engage in some entertainment pursuits, although he often did so as part of his official duties. For example, in a 1782 letter to Edmund Pendleton he described his attendance at a public function to entertain the minister of France. He noted that "it was deemed politic at this crisis to display every proper evidence of attachment to our ally." He also stated that after the initial reception of the French minister, "a public entertainment followed, and fireworks at night closed the scene."[84]

By this point some readers may have formed an image of Madison as ceaselessly sitting indoors pouring over boring books that would drive anyone else bonkers, while his only entertainment was attendance at equally boring government functions. Many would assume that a personality immersed in that much boredom must be as dry and flat as an old dog bone.

But nothing could be further from the truth. Historian Saul K. Padover shocked his readers in his 1953 book 'The Complete Madison' by noting that while Jefferson was rather dull in social gatherings, Madison frequently cracked jokes and sincerely seemed to enjoy making people smile.[85] Padover was not the only historian who noted this difference. One historian commented on the personality difference between Madison and Jefferson in describing what occurred when Jefferson visited Madison's home at Montpelier: "At meals Jefferson, whose sense of humor was not strong, enjoyed Madison's drollery. Out the long dining room windows laughter floated. (It was through one of them that Madison, once, having tilted his chair too far, fell out backward)."[86]

Contrary to the stodgy image that has come to be associated with him, Madison was "capable of jollity and possessed a fund of amusing stories." Sir Augustus Foster, British Minister to Washington during Madison's presidency, noted that Madison was "a social, jovial, and good-humoured companion, full of anecdote."[87] James K. Paulding, a friend of

Madison, stated that "He was a man of wit, relished wit in others, and his small bright blue eyes would twinkle most wickedly, when lighted up by some whimsical conception." Another example of Madison's playfulness and humor, although undoubtedly motivated by relief from the tremendous stress of office, was when Madison was on his way home to Montpelier in April 1817 after leaving the presidency. He was observed being "as playful as a child; talked and joked with everybody on board, and ... [was like] a schoolboy on a long vacation."[88]

Perhaps it was this odd quirk of his unique personality that led to one of the most unusual partnerships of all time--the marriage of the supposedly dry and dull James Madison to super socialite Dolly Payne Todd. In May, 1794, Madison asked Aaron Burr to introduce him to the attractive and vivacious Dolly, who had taken Philadelphia by storm and was much sought after by many anxious suitors. Dolly's reaction upon hearing of the requested introduction shows her surprise at Madison's attention. She sent a quick note to her niece, Elizabeth Collins, saying "Thou must come to me--Aaron Burr says that the great little Madison has asked to be brought to see me this evening."[89]

The official gossip chain in the capital was captivated as the courtship progressed. Even without modern tabloids at the checkout line of grocery stores to scream the news, everyone knew that Madison was smitten by Dolly and was actively courting her. And everyone but the couple themselves seemed to know they were engaged even before they were. Indeed, at one point first lady Martha Washington summoned Dolly to meet her, and asked her bluntly "is it true that you are engaged to James Madison?" Dolly responded "I think not." Martha then let her know in clear terms that both she and the President would heartily support such a union if it ever progressed from gossip to reality.[90]

And progress it did. To escape the maelstrom of speculation, Dolly retired to a relative's home in Virginia. Madison was not far behind her, and love blossomed. In September the couple were married at Harewood, Virginia. Not long after they returned to the nation's capital at Philadelphia, where they resided at 115 Spruce Street, turning it into one of the social centers of the city. Said one historian: "Madison's home was open always during the congressional session for entertainment. Dolly was required to receive the great and small of the government and distinguished foreign visitors."[91] Another historian had this to say about Dolly's new role as the wife of a prominent congressman: "Her new environment contained balls and parades and festivals attending the opening of Congress or the birthday of George Washington; there were dances, plays, and visits."[92] Naturally, James Madison participated in these events as well. This hardly sounds like a man who hated entertainment. Rather, he was a man who knew how to keep it in perspective, and knew what so many in America today seem to have forgotten--that entertainment should be pursued energetically but sparingly, and never as an end in itself.

And then came the 'revolution' of 1800 when John Adams was turned out of the White House and Jefferson became its new master. To the surprise of no one, he brought his good friend James Madison on board as his Secretary of State. And it took little time for Jefferson to realize how invaluable Madison's wife Dolly was as a hostess--especially since Jefferson was a widower. As one historian noted, "Dolly had an unmatched ability to make guests feel at home." But she was not the only popular one at the President's social gatherings. "Madison too pleased people. His wit sparkled and his anecdotes were often side splitting ... he showed unfailing good humor and a strong relish for the ludicrous." Dolly loved his stories. "Jemmy's tales were so good, she always said, they were worth hearing again."[93]

For 16 long years, during the respective eight year presidential terms of both Jefferson and Madison, Dolly served as hostess at the White House, and James Madison as its unofficial comedian. No visit to official Washington was complete without stopping in at the Madison's. Even after the capital was burned by the British, the Madisons kept up their active social calendar at their new residence at the Octagon House in Foggy Bottom. The simple fact is, if anyone knew entertainment--both its value, and how to keep it in perspective and not overdo it--it was James and Dolly Madison. We would do well to take a lesson from their example today.

The word that best sums up this attitude toward entertainment, and indeed toward maintaining balance in all aspects of life, is 'temperance.' Contrary to popular belief, this term has little to do with a movement to end the consumption of alcohol. Rather, temperance is a way of looking at and living life with balance, juggling work, family obligations, community service and entertainment in a careful manner that never accentuates one above the other, and which keeps all in perspective. James Madison became a master of this art in his long life. Indeed, his success at living temperately is summed up by comments from one of his servants: "I never saw him in a passion and never knew him to strike a slave ... neither would he allow an overseer to do it ... He was temperate in his habits."[94] Madison once offered a toast that nicely summed up his temperate attitude toward life, which he made during the visit of the celebrated Revolutionary War hero Lafayette to Jefferson's home in Monticello. He said, "Happy the people who have virtue for their guest and gratitude for their feast."[95]

After leaving the White House, Madison maintained his sense of balance upon returning to the life of a farmer at Montpelier. A constant stream of visitors made it difficult to give his crops the attention they deserved. But Madison politely never turned his visitors away. Like so many who visited Washington during Dolly's heyday of 16 years, visitors came away having experienced entertainment and hospitality at their best. James' stories and Dolly's hosting were absolutely captivating. And because of this, the visitors to Montpelier did not diminish over the years.

For all this, Madison loved to get away from visitors at times. Indeed, he commented in a 1794 letter to Horatio Gates about one of his very favorite pastimes--travel. This was an unusual interest for perhaps the only statesman of his age who never went abroad. "Let me recommend the best medicine in the world," he said, "a long journey, at a mild season, through a pleasant country, in easy stages."[96] One can only imagine that if Madison were alive today, he would be seen taking frequent cruises to exotic destinations, finding joy not only in the journey but also in learning more about the cultures and peoples he was fortunate enough to visit.

Temperate to the end, it is reported that even in death, Madison saw both the interesting and fascinating aspects of learning. Death for him would be but one more wonderful discovery. In late June of 1836, his favorite niece, Nelly Willis, was watching Madison eat his breakfast when she noticed a slight change of expression cross his face. "Was anything wrong?" she asked. He replied, "Nothing more than a change of mind, my dear." And then "his head instantly dropped, and he ceased breathing as quickly as the snuff of a candle goes out."[97]

NOTES:

[81] Padover, at 3.

[82] 1 Hunt, at 20.

[83] Id. at 57.

[84] Id. at 194.

[85] Padover, at 8-9.

[86] Virginia Moore, The Madisons, 90 (1979).

[87] Padover at 8-9.

[88] Ralph L. Ketcham ed., "An Unpublished Sketch of James Madison by James K. Paulding," 67 Virginia Magazine of History and Biography 432-437 (1959).

[89] Allen C. Clark, Life and Letters of Dolly Madison, 19 (1914).

[90] Id. at 20.

[91] Katharine Anthony, Dolly Madison: Her Life and Times 94 (1949).

[92] David B. Mattern & Holly C. Shulman, The Selected Letters of Dolly Payne Madison, 17 (2003).

[93] Id. at 159-160.

[94] Padover at 10-11.

[95] Brandt at 616.

[96] William T. Hutchinson ed., 15 The Papers of James Madison, 164 (1991).

[97] Jack N. Rakove, James Madison and the Creation of the American Republic, 218 (2d ed., 2002).

CHAPTER EIGHT
Religious Freedom

One of the chief causes championed by Madison throughout his life was religious liberty. With undeviating consistency he spoke out strongly against governmental bias and oppression of religious groups, and of any laws or actions that belittled or attacked the religious beliefs of others. One of the earliest examples of this is found in a letter Madison wrote to his friend William Bradford in January, 1774 when Madison was only 22. His disgust for religious bigotry is clearly expounded--a disgust that never left him, and was a byword for the remainder of his life:

"There are at this time in the adjacent country not less than five or six well-meaning men in close jail for publishing their religious sentiments, which in the main are very orthodox. I have neither patience to hear, talk or think of anything relative to this matter; for I have squabbled and scolded, abused and ridiculed so long about it to little purpose, that I am without common patience. So I must beg you to pity me, and pray for liberty of conscience to all."[98]

A few months later Madison again wrote to Bradford about the religious bigotry that existed even in the Virginia legislature. He noted "Petitions, I hear, are already forming among the persecuted Baptists, and I fancy it is in the thoughts of the Presbyterians also, to intercede for greater liberty in matters of religion. For my own part, I cannot help being very doubtful of their succeeding in the attempt." Much of the fault for this lay with the established clergy of the official Anglican Church, who were trying to use the legislature to secure their positions. Madison stated: "The clergy are a numerous and powerful body, have great influence at home by reason of their connection with and dependence on the Bishops and crown, and will naturally employ all their art and interest to depress their rising adversaries; for such they must consider dissenters who rob them of the good will of the people, and may in time endanger their livings and security." He concluded by pessimistically noting that "Religious bondage shackles and debilitates the mind, and unfits it for every noble enterprise."[99]

Up to this time, Madison's concerns about religious persecution represented a personal struggle, since he was a mere young citizen with little capacity to do anything about it. But by the summer of 1776, Madison found himself serving in the Virginia House of Delegates, and was on a committee to form a new constitution and declaration of rights. Now was his chance to make a difference. Yet, young and inexperienced as he was, Madison largely yielded to the work of George Mason on the committee, who did most of the writing on these important documents. The only instance where Madison rose to contradict the senior Mr. Mason had to do with the clause in the Declaration of Rights on religious freedom. Mason proposed the following wording: "That religion, or the duty which we owe to our creator, and the manner of discharging it, can be directed only by reason and conviction, not by force or violence; and therefore that all men *should enjoy the fullest toleration in the exercise of religion,* according to the dictates of conscience ..." Madison objected to the italicized portion and its use of the word "toleration," since he and everyone else knew this only meant that religions other than the 'official' Anglican church would merely be 'tolerated.' This was the very point Madison had raised with his friend William Bradford two years earlier. Something more than 'toleration' was needed--something like equal rights. Accordingly, Madison suggested a change in the wording to read "... that all men are equally entitled to the full and free exercise of it [religion] according to the dictates of conscience ..." The delegates agreed to this change, although they refused Madison's additional suggestion that "no man or class of men ought, on account of religion be invested with peculiar emoluments or privileges," since this was too direct of an attack on the official Anglican Church.[100]

It is significant that Madison's very first effort in the work of government was this wording to promote religious freedom. There really was no issue he felt stronger about. And the impact of his contribution was great. The Virginia Declaration of Rights was considered a landmark document that was heavily copied by other states for years as they formed their own Bills and Declarations of Rights. Madison's simple change of wording went a long way.

Perhaps Madison hoped the new statement in the Virginia Declaration of Rights would finally bring an end to official religious bigotry by the legislature. Unfortunately, this was not the case, as the Virginia legislature ignored this clear declaration a mere eight years later--contributing to Madison's view that Declarations of Rights are mere "parchment barriers" which the legislature would often ignore at will. In 1784 while Madison was in the Virginia House of Delegates he opposed a bill which would require "a tax of _____ percent on all taxable property for the support of teachers of the Christian religion. Each person when he pays his tax is to name the society to which he dedicates it, and in case of refusal to do so, the tax is to be applied to the maintenance of a school in the County ... it is chiefly obnoxious on account of its dishonorable principle and dangerous tendency."[101] The 'dangerous tendency' of course was mixing of church and state since tax dollars were to go directly to the support of "Christian" churches. Madison's notes for his speech against this bill give his views on religious freedom in general, and his concerns about the behavior of organized religion in particular. His abbreviated notes include the following blunt statements: "Religion not within purview of civil authority ... True question--not is religion necessary, but are religious establishments necessary for religion? No ... experience shews religion corrupted by establishments ..."[102] It should be noted that

Madison was no atheist, but devoutly attended the Anglican Church himself. Accordingly, he firmly believed that religion itself was worthy of government protection. However, he strongly disagreed with government protection of a specific church's version of religion, since this elevated the favored church above others. For Madison, this distinction between governmental protection of religion generally but not of specific churches was crucial, and made all the difference.

The chief difficulty Madison had with the 1784 proposed tax for churches in Virginia was that it applied only to "Christian religions," and courts would be called upon to interpret the statute and define just what a "Christian religion" was. Besides the obvious prejudice against non-Christian religions, the law created potential problems among religions that claimed to be "Christian," but in the view of their opponents were not. Madison's abbreviated notes express his concerns about this potential problem: "What is Christianity? Courts of Law to judge. What edition [of scriptures]: Hebrew, Septuagint or Vulgate? What copy what translation? What books canonical, what apocryphal? ... In what light are they to be viewed, as dictated every letter by inspiration, or the essential parts only? ... if some doctrines be essential to Christianity those who reject these, whatever name they take are no Christian society? Is it Trinitarianism, Arianism, Socinianism? Is it salvation by faith or works also, by free grace or by will, &c., &c. What clue is to guide [a] Judge thro' this labyrinth when ye question comes before them whether any particular society is a Christian society?" Madison's conclusion was that such a law "dishonors Christianity."[103]

Some may wonder why Madison was so concerned with what seems to be exceedingly fine distinctions. After all, just how hard can it be to define what a "Christian" Church is, and what it is not? Yet, in expressing this concern, Madison was once more prophetic, since this is a debate that continues to this day. Consider the 2012 presidential candidacy of avowed "Mormon" Mitt Romney. Many opponents in the religious right firmly asserted that "Mormons" are not Christians--handily ignoring the reality that the official name of the "Mormon" Church is "The Church of Jesus Christ of Latter-day Saints," and that "Mormons" proclaim Christ as the divine son of God who alone offers salvation to mankind. The apparent justification for labeling Mormons as "non-Christian" was that Mormons eschew the common protestant view of salvation solely by grace, and assert that effort and works are necessary for saving grace to apply--exactly as Madison predicted! Yet, as

Madison pointed out, is this a justifiable distinction? Just how is a "Christian" to be defined, after all? And is it proper for government to get involved in such fanciful efforts?

Although Madison opposed the Virginia church-tax law with vigor, for a time it looked like his efforts were doomed to fail. The law was initially approved in the Virginia House of Delegates by a vote of 47 to 32. Fortunately however, the final vote that would turn the bill into law was deferred to a later date. Clearly there was much work for Madison to do in the meantime to overcome the religious intolerance and bigotry he saw all around him, and which sometimes surfaced into actual laws like this.

Madison was pleased that opposition gradually increased against the proposed law. He noted in an August 20, 1785 letter to Jefferson that "the opposition to the general assessment gains ground. At the instance of some of its adversaries I drew up the remonstrance hereby enclosed." The "remonstrance" Madison referred to is his greatest statement on religious freedom, regarding the essential necessity of keeping the church and state completely separate. Officially entitled "Memorial and Remonstrance Against Religious Assessments," the document was written as a petition to be signed by those opposing final passage of the law. Madison noted that "it has been sent thro' the medium of confidential persons in a number of the upper counties, and I am told will be pretty extensively signed."[104]

In the Memorial and Remonstrance, Madison first noted the irony of civil government becoming involved in religious matters, since "before any man can be considered as a member of civil society, he must be considered as a subject of the Governor of the Universe." This once again shows that Madison was deeply religious in his personal views, and was certainly no anti-religious atheist. For Madison, the relationship of God to man predated and was superior to any relationship between man and man as codified in government, or even between man and church. Therefore, for government to usurp the right to interfere with that prior relationship between God and man was a specious claim with no foundation whatever. It would be akin to a group of playground children at school dictating how each child in the group was to interact with his parents. While God patiently and tolerantly does not send down immediate lightning bolts to zap legislators who pass such laws, that does not make it right for the majority in the legislature to, as Madison said, "trespass on the rights of the minority."

But Madison was just warming up in his Memorial and Remonstrance. He bluntly stated that legislators who make laws favoring some religions over others "exceed the commission from which they derive their authority, and are tyrants. The people who submit to it are governed by laws made neither by themselves, nor by an authority derived from them, and are slaves." Then Madison asked a very telling question: "Who does not see that the same authority which can establish Christianity, in exclusion of all other religions, may establish with the same ease any particular sect of Christians, in exclusion of all other sects?"[105]

These are highly relevant issues, even today. Many in America believe that since Christianity in America's heritage has been so fundamental a force, it should be given pre-eminent respect. While recognition of America's historical Christian heritage can be a worthy endeavor, any official preference by government of Christian religions over non-Christian ones would fly in the face of that standard of religious liberty the founders espoused. Hence, a city-owned nativity scene to be set up in the town park at Christmas is improper--unless of course the city also sets up a Jewish Candellabra, and other scenes representative of other non-Christian sects. The suggestion of setting up such a multitude of scenes in the park is, of course, absurd. In short, there is no harm in a legislator proclaiming himself a Christian, but if he supports a law that gives preference to Christian religious beliefs while subjugating or ignoring the religious views of non-Christians, he has crossed the line into forbidden territory.

Madison would concur in this, as he eloquently stated in his Memorial and Remonstrance. "Whilst we assert for ourselves a freedom to embrace, to profess and to observe the religion which we believe to be of divine origin, we cannot deny an equal freedom to those whose minds have not yet yielded to the evidence which has convinced us. If this freedom be abused, it is an offense against God, not against man: To God, therefore, not to men, must an account of it be rendered." Indeed, Madison noted that the law actually hurt the cause of Christians, since it would "foster in those who still reject [Christianity] a suspicion that its friends are too conscious of its fallacies to trust to its own merits."[106]

For Madison, such a law would unavoidably bring about the very effect it was seeking to avoid--in the name of religious tolerance, it would arouse religious bigotry and contention. "Torrents of blood have been spilt in the old world by vain attempts of the secular arm [government] to extinguish Religious discord, by proscribing [preventing] all difference in Religious opinion ... The very appearance of the bill has transformed that 'Christian forbearance, love and charity' which of late mutually prevailed, into animosities and jealousies, which may not soon be appeased."

For Madison, the Christian tax law was a frightening demonstration that the Virginia legislature apparently thought it had supreme authority over rights. If religion could be meddled with by the legislature, in open defiance of the 1776 Declaration of Rights, could not the legislature also abuse rights of free speech or of the press? Such legislative arrogance and control threatened to "sweep away all our fundamental rights." Once again, Madison says it best in his own words:

"Either we must say that they may control the freedom of the press, may abolish the trial by jury, may swallow up the Executive and Judiciary powers of the state; nay, that they may despoil us of our very right of suffrage, and erect themselves into an independent and hereditary assembly: or we must say that they have no authority to enact into law the bill under consideration."[107]

To the gratification of Madison and others who opposed the tax assessment bill, it was defeated when it came up for final vote in the next session of the Virginia legislature.

Another example of improper mixing of church and state arose at roughly the same time as the Virginia church-tax law, only this time at the national level. Fortunately however, it did not involve a similar protracted debate. In a letter to James Monroe dated May 29, 1785, Madison expressed satisfaction that the Continental Congress had turned down a proposed federal law pertaining to public lands sold by the government which would set "apart a district of land in each Township for supporting the religion of the majority of inhabitants." Madison then let his feelings flow: "How a regulation so unjust in itself, so foreign to the authority of Congress, so hurtful to the sale of the public land, and smelling so strongly of an antiquated bigotry could have received the countenance of a [Committee] is truly [a] matter of astonishment."[108]

Three years later, in 1788, during the great debate in Virginia over ratification of the new federal constitution, Madison once again had the opportunity to discuss his ideas on religious freedom and the best way to maintain it. These comments show that Madison, ever the pragmatist, did not see government mandated solutions as the best ones. Rather, societal solutions were better, since the attitudes of the people tend to regulate their conduct better than a mere law which can be ignored. He said:

"Is a bill of rights a security for religion? ... If there were a majority of one sect, a bill of rights would be a poor protection for liberty. Happily for the states, they enjoy the utmost freedom of religion. This freedom arises from that multiplicity of sects which pervades America, and which is the best and only security for religious liberty in any society. For where there is such a variety of sects, there cannot be a majority of any one sect to oppress and persecute the rest ... There is not a shadow of right in the general government to intermeddle with religion. Its least interference with it would be a most flagrant usurpation."[109]

For Madison, private religious belief was "the most sacred of all property."[110] Throughout his long political career, he was constantly watching to make sure new laws did not improperly meddle in religion. No wonder then that ten years later in 1798, Madison's objection to the Alien and Sedition Acts under the Adams administration included an argument about religion. It will be recalled that these acts allowed for the deportation or imprisonment of persons for expressing opinions against the administration. Madison decried the act at length, noting among other things that

"Opinions as well as facts are made punishable ... By subjecting the truth of opinion to the regulation, fine and imprisonment, to be inflicted by those who are of a different opinion, the free range of the human mind is injuriously restrained. The sacred obligations of religion flow from the due exercise of opinion, in the solemn discharge of which man is accountable to his God alone ... This law then commits the ... sacrilege ... of placing in a state of danger the free exercise of religious opinions."[111]

He also noted that "under it men of a particular religious opinion might be excluded from office ... and under it Congress might denominate a religion to be heretical and licentious, and proceed to its suppression."[112]

Madison took offense when any religious entity was criticized, even if the religion at issue was not one he believed in personally. Hence, during a debate on new immigration laws, one congressman "ridiculed certain tenets of the Catholic religion." Madison promptly rose and stated "he did not approve the ridicule attempted to be thrown out on the Roman Catholics. In their religion there was nothing inconsistent with the purest Republicanism ... Americans had no right to ridicule Catholics. They had, many of them, proved good citizens during the Revolution."[113]

With a background such as this, it comes as no surprise that Madison avowed in his first inaugural address that one of his goals as president was "to avoid the slightest interference with the rights of conscience or the functions of religion, so wisely exempted from civil jurisdiction."[114] In February, 1811, he demonstrated his commitment to this principal when he vetoed an act of Congress "incorporating the Protestant Episcopal Church in the ... District of Columbia." This was Madison's own church! Yet he vetoed the law, noting that "the bill exceeds the rightful authority to which governments are limited by the essential distinction between civil and religious functions." Just as he entered into the Presidential chair with an avowal of maintaining a separation of church and state and protecting religious freedom--and proved that he meant it by his 1811 veto--Madison ended his presidential service with a charge in his 1816 annual message to Congress to "interdict against encroachments and compacts between religion and the state."[115]

Madison never relinquished his zeal for religious toleration throughout the remainder of his life. Indeed, in 1818 he provided a key insight into one of the reasons he had so long and arduously fought for religious toleration and freedom. In a letter responding to Mordecai M. Noah's statement that the Jews of America owed many of their blessings to Madison and his colleagues, Madison stated

"Having ever regarded the freedom of religious opinions and worship as equally belonging to every sect, and the secure enjoyment of it as the best human provision for bringing all either into the same way of thinking or into that mutual charity which is the only substitute, I observe with pleasure the view you give of the spirit in which your sect partake of the blessings offered by our government and laws."[116]

For Madison then, religion represented an aspiration for charity, brotherhood and kindness--the very ingredients needed for religious toleration. Any attempt by officials of government to give benefits to one religion above others was the opposite of such charitable, religious feeling. In short, government sponsorship of religion was anti-religious, and threatened all the rights of the people. No wonder then that Madison concluded a discussion of the religions in Virginia with the observation that "the number, the industry and the morality of the Priesthood, and the devotion of the people have been manifestly increased by the total separation of the Church from the state."[117] And in 1822 he noted that in Virginia, "religion prevails with more zeal and a more exemplary priesthood than it ever did when established and patronized by Public authority." As he bluntly stated on that occasion, "religion and government will both exist in greater purity the less they are mixed together."[118]

NOTES:

[98] 1 Hunt, at 21.

[99] Ibid at 22-24.

[100] Merrill D. Peterson ed., The Founding Fathers: James Madison, a Biography in His Own Words, 40-42 (1974).

[101] 2 Hunt, at 113-114.

[102] Ibid at 88.

[103] Ibid at 89.

[104] Ibid at 163.

[105] Ibid at 185-186.

[106] Ibid at 186-187.

[107] Ibid at 191.

[108] Ibid at 145.

[109] 5 Hunt, at 176.

[110] 6 Hunt, at 102.

[111] Ibid at 337

[112] Ibid at 335.

[113] Ibid at 231.

[114] 8 Hunt, at 49.

[115] Ibid at 132, 384.

[116] Ibid at 412.

[117] Ibid at 432.

[118] 9 Hunt at 102.

CHAPTER NINE
Madison's Prophetic Views on Other Issues

Visionary that he was, Madison saw a good deal more in America's future than what has been described in this book so far. We have already seen his clear-sighted vision in areas of rights, war and foreign policy, finances, entertainment and religious freedom, so it should come as no surprise that he was equally visionary in respect to additional issues that he knew would affect the country someday. This chapter will describe his vision regarding just a few of these matters.

One of the most impressive demonstrations of Madison's genius and prophetic insight is found in his final message to Congress in the fall of 1816. In that address he discussed a number of issues that he knew would soon face America, and urged a consistent and fair way to deal with these issues. One historian captures the scope and breadth of his vision: "Madison's final message to Congress was on the face of it an impossible list of requests. In reality it was a blueprint for the American future. He asked for a decimal [metric] system of weights and measures--not yet achieved; a revision of the criminal code (accomplished in 1825); a Department of the Interior (created in 1849); federal aid to education (begun in 1862); a system of appellate courts (established in 1911)."[119] Clearly, Madison saw a good deal more in America's future than most Americans did. And he also saw the various governmental departments that would be needed to help bring about the brighter future he envisioned.

But this was not all. Shortly after this, Madison gave an incredibly insightful view of the importance of preserving the environment, and the danger the nation would face if they failed to do so. This warning predated what we consider to be modern environmental concerns by more than 150 years! He stated, "We can scarcely be warranted in supposing that all the productive powers of its [earth's] surface can be made subservient to the use of man, in exclusion of all the plants and animals." He went on to say that

"The earth contains not less than thirty or forty thousand kinds of plants; not less than six or seven hundred of birds; not less than three or four hundred of quadrupeds; to say nothing of the thousand species of fishes. Of reptiles and insects there are more than can be numbered ... On comparing this vast profusion and multiplicity of beings with the few grains and grasses, the few herbs and roots, and the few fowls and quadrupeds, which make up the short list adapted to the wants of man; it is difficult to believe that it lies with him so to remodel the work of nature ... by a destruction not only of individuals but of entire species."

Madison strongly objected to this "multiplication of the human race at the expense of the rest of the organized creation." He then observed the danger of killing off trees and forests, in words that would be approved by modern environmentalists concerned with the loss of the Amazon rainforests. "When our ancestors arrived they found the trees of the forest the great obstacle to their settlement and cultivation. The great effort was of course to destroy the trees. It would seem that they contracted and transmitted an antipathy to them; for the trees were not even spared around the dwellings, where their shade would have been a comfort and their beauty an ornament." The loss related to far more than lack of wood to keep fires burning, but to the very atmosphere and air. Madison explained it thus:

"It seems to be now well understood that the atmosphere, when respired by animals, becomes unfitted for their further use, and [conversely] fitted for the absorption of vegetables; and that when evolved by the latter, it is refitted for the respiration of the former; an interchange being thus kept up, by which this breath of life is received by each ... May it not be concluded from this admirable arrangement and beautiful feature in the economy of nature, that if the whole class of ... vegetables were extinguished, the use of it [the atmosphere] by the animal class alone would deprive it of its fitness for their support?"[120]

In the same discourse in which he provided these environmental insights, Madison gave his views on farming. As proprietor of Montpelier, Madison had been studying farming and applying farm techniques all his life. Few today think of Madison as a farmer, but he was one of the most knowledgeable on the subject of his age. One historian noted the forward-thinking nature of his farm comments in these words:

"He advocated contour plowing and horizontal planting of slopes, greater use of manures and composts, rotation of crops, noncultivation of inferior land, improved breeding of livestock, avoidance of grass and forest fires, reduction of timber cutting, reforestation. In short, he advocated and practiced the methods of farming taken up as new and revolutionary by government agencies more than a century later."[121]

But there are more examples than these of Madison's forward-thinking genius. For example, in 1825 he commented on the workability of a society in Indiana which was formed on the basis of socialism. Little knowing that he was predicting the economic woes of communist nations more than 100 years later, Madison noted that a socialist enclave would rise no higher than the economic status of the surrounding communities. In his post-presidential years Madison also spoke of joint federal/state projects for improvements, suggesting that the costs should be divided between the two governmental entities. By this novel idea, "the vast modern system of federal aid to states was thus foreshadowed." As for controversies between the boundaries of state and federal power, such matters were to be decided by the Supreme Court.[122] This was not an altogether popular idea in Madison's day, in which states rights were greater than they are today. But Madison foresaw the need for the federal judiciary to be superior in such matters. As we saw in chapter 3, he never contemplated for the Supreme Court to become legislatively active in social matters and rights issues better decided by the legislature. But when it came to legitimate structural controversies such as those arising between federal and state power, the Supreme Court was the best body to decide such disputes.

The ultimate state/federal issue of his day of course was slavery. Like Washington and Jefferson before him, Madison was paradoxically both a Virginia slave owner and an opponent of slavery. As early as 1783, he expressed unwillingness to punish a runaway slave "for coveting that liberty for which we have paid the price of so much blood and have proclaimed so often to be the right and worthy pursuit of every human being."[123] Instead, Madison sold the slave in Philadelphia where he knew he would go free in seven years under Pennsylvania law.

At the Constitutional Convention Madison noted that "We have seen the mere distinction of color made in the most enlightened period of time, a ground of the most oppressive dominion ever exercised by man over man."[124] The convention notes for August 25, 1787 indicate that "Mr. Madison thought it wrong to admit in the Constitution the idea that there could be property in men."[125] In an 1825 letter to Francis Wright he wrote, "The magnitude of this evil among us is so deeply felt, and so universally acknowledged, that no merit could be greater than that of devising a satisfactory remedy for it." Interestingly, he did not feel it was very difficult for government to find a way for slaves to gradually become free, and felt that gradual change in this regard would be better and easier for people to adjust to than a single great event of emancipation which he prophetically felt could lead to war. "If emancipation was the sole object, the extinguishment of slavery would be easy, cheap and complete. The purchase by the public of all female children at their birth, leaving them in bondage till it would defray the cost of rearing them, would within a limited period" erase slavery from the nation.[126] This idea was extremely creative, since a free black female would naturally have free children. From a purely practical standpoint the plan was genius of course, since it would cost the nation nothing, while gradually forcing the drastic change to society and the economy that the end of slavery would bring about.

But genius as he was, Madison knew that freeing the slaves was only half the problem. The other and far more difficult half had to do with civil rights, and the extent to which a black nonslave would be truly as free as his white contemporaries. In this regard, he foresaw the racial tensions and civil rights movement more than 100 years in America's future. With his usual prophetic insight Madison believed that if the freed slaves stayed where they were they would "change only from one to another species of oppression." As one historian noted, "Madison's portrait of free blacks in a hostile white society might have been put on paper 150 years later" with the civil rights battles of the 1960s.[127]

Because Madison saw these difficulties, he was convinced it was better for former slaves to go somewhere they could feel freer and not suffer oppression from their former masters and other whites. Obviously, the proud and vain whites, with their greater amounts of money and power, were not about to be the ones to move away, and yield their homes to the blacks. Nor were these whites about to accept freed blacks as equals, even though that is what they obviously should have done. Due to the biases of his day, Madison doubted whether blacks and whites would ever learn to peacefully co-exist, and therefore favored creation of Liberia in Africa, or the relocation of former slaves to Caribbean islands, or to the unpopulated west. The problem was, as he himself admitted, that "among the slaves there is an almost universal preference of their present condition [of slavery] to freedom in a distant and unknown land."[128]

As the issue of slavery became more and more polarized between northern and southern states, Madison became increasingly alarmed at southerners who threatened to secede from the union. He said, "It is painful to observe the unceasing efforts to alarm the South by imputations against the North of unconstitutional designs on the subject of the slaves." He expounded further as to why he felt the issue was emotionalized more in the South than in the North, at least in his day:

"I have no doubt in believing that no such intermeddling disposition exists in the body of our Northern brethren. Their good faith is sufficiently guarantied by the interest they have as merchants, as ship owners, and as manufacturers, in preserving a union with the slaveholding states. On the other hand, what madness in the South to look for greater safety in disunion. It would be worse than jumping out of the Frying-pan into the fire; it would be jumping into the fire for fear of the Frying-pan."[129]

Madison was particularly troubled by frequent use by secessionists of his and Jefferson's Kentucky and Virginia resolutions, which were written in 1798 against the Alien and Sedition Acts of the Adams administration. Secession was proposed by South Carolina in 1832-1833, due to its opposition to a new federal tariff law. Madison opposed this effort, and was fully aware that the same arguments for secession would likely be used by Southern states as years passed, due to slavery. For this reason during his final years he wrote repeatedly on this subject, stating again and again that his purpose for authoring the Virginia Resolution was to merely express the disapproval of his state with the Federal Alien and Sedition Acts, but nothing more. It would be similar to a Western state today expressing disapproval over federal retention of federal lands, or an expression of disapproval by any state with any act of Congress. The intention was never to promote secession from the union, which to Madison was unthinkable. Indeed, in drafting the Virginia resolution Madison had taken great pains to avoid wording that might even remotely suggest secession as an option. For him it simply was not, and never could be. Unfortunately, his friend Jefferson in his Kentucky resolution was not as careful in his wording, which is why secessionists more frequently quoted Jefferson.

Again, Madison was greatly concerned over the increasing division he saw in America between North and South over the issue of slavery. It is therefore not surprising that in 1819 he predicted conflict if such a condition continued. What caused his concern was the increasing polarization around admitting new states into the union as either slave or free. Madison said:

"The tendency of what has passed and what is passing [regarding the admission of slave and free states] fills me with no slight anxiety. Parties under some denominations or other must always be expected in a government as free as ours. When the individuals belonging to them are intermingled in every part of the whole Country, they strengthen the union of the whole, while they divide every part. [However] Should a state of parties arise, founded on geographical boundaries and other physical and permanent distinctions which happen to coincide with them, what is to control these great repulsive masses from awful shocks against each other?"[130]

Truly, Madison was able to see into the future, and foresee the significant difficulties his beloved country would likely face in the years to come. He foresaw the civil war, racial prejudice, environmental destruction and a host of other calamities. But he always saw more than this as well. He also saw the way to resolve these difficulties, if people were simply willing to do so. While his prophetic genius never failed him, our unwillingness to be guided by it has repeatedly failed us. And in this, we have ignored his wisdom to our own folly and condemnation.

NOTES:

[119] Brandt, at 600.

[120] James Madison, "An address delivered before the Agricultural Society of Albermarle, (Va.) on Tuesday, May 12, 1819, found in Edmund Ruffin ed., 5 The Farmer's Register, No. 7, 413-414, 422 (1837). Madison had been named President of the Society.

[121] Brandt at 609.

[122] Ibid at 616, 623, 628.

[123] 1 Hunt at Introduction, xxiv.

[124] 3 Hunt at 104.

[125] 4 Hunt at 305-306.

[126] 9 Hunt at 224-225, 498.

[127] Brandt at 611.

[128] 9 Hunt at 500.

[129] Ibid at 517.

[130] 9 Hunt at 12.

JAMES MADISON.

CHAPTER TEN
Conclusion

James Madison saw our day. With prophetic insight he saw the struggles that would likely result from the weaknesses he perceived in the constitution, the government, and in the American people themselves. He had tremendous predictive power, as he contemplated the conflicts that would most probably come over the definition and source of rights, money matters, war and international relations, racism, entertainment, religious freedom--all the issues that marked his day, and continue to mark ours as fraught with challenge and difficulty.

He was a prophet and a prophet SEES. But what the prophet sees in respect to problems coming in the future is less important than what he sees as the solutions to those problems. If we merely look at Madison to marvel at his prophetic genius and his incredible ability to foresee problems and challenges that would happen in the future, we are missing the point. What we mainly need to notice are the solutions he foresaw and the things we can do to extract ourselves from the messes we have gotten ourselves into. If we fail to pay sufficient attention to these things, his prophetic vision will avail us nothing.

And what did he see that we should do? Plenty. He saw that our fixation with rights issues would not be solved by the Supreme Court, since such issues are societal and moral ones that cannot be judicially mandated. He knew that we need to respect and strictly follow the natural rights views of the founding generation. But he also knew that if we are unwilling to do this and are foolish enough to defy natural law and try to re-define rights, such questions are best decided by the people themselves through their elected representatives, rather than the courts.

The judicial activism that has evolved regarding rights today seems insuperable--but it is not. All we need to do is return to Madison's original vision. We should simply acknowledge and strictly follow the original intent and natural rights views of the founding generation. But if we are unwilling to do this, then we should at least find a way--by constitutional amendment if necessary--to re-enthrone the legislature as the body with the final say in rights issues other than those involving the criminally accused. Such an amendment would be based on Madison's legislative veto model, and would provide for a new kind of 'veto'--one by Congress of a non-criminal rights decision by the Supreme Court.[131] If we follow the founders' views of natural rights, or at least shift the final word on rights issues back to the people, we will be on much safer ground.

What else did he see? A modern obsession with foreign affairs that too frequently follows a path either of appeasement or of over-involvement. Madison's war presidency highlighted the need to try to avoid war, but not at any cost. For the government to truly maintain its sovereign rights, there may come a time that talks end and shooting starts. No country can ever yield this ultimate fall-back position. But once again, such an event was never intended to be the decision of a single man. Congress, as the voice of the people, must ultimately decide on such a somber matter. The president should never overstep his constitutional bounds or commit the troops without the support of the people. And even after the troops are committed, he and the government at large must sacredly protect the ongoing right of opponents of war to express their views.

There is much else that he saw that can be of aid to us. He saw the glut, loss of confidence and needless waste that result from over taxation. His prophetic solution to this was simple--just put an end to it and return to the transparency of justifying expenditures before they are expended, just like a business must do. He saw both the danger and necessity of banks, and how we must watch them closely. He saw the need for government to exercise both charity and firmness towards its citizens--charity toward the innocent and the workers, firmness toward those who seek to glut themselves at the hands of the deserving. And he saw the need to re-enthrone honesty and frugality as financial touchstones in the operation of government.

Madison saw a good deal more than this of course. He saw the waste and silliness that result when people become obsessed with endless entertainment, and fail to discipline themselves and be temperate. He saw the danger that comes when government meddles with religion, and the need to constantly be on guard against any laws by which one religious creed is preferred over another. He saw the need to actively try to preserve our environment, and our need to avoid any pattern in society that tends to enslave a part of the people unfairly. All of these he saw as both warnings and opportunities for us, if we will but heed his counsel.

For Madison truly saw our day. As the foremost of the founding prophets, his vision has transcended the centuries and still stands solid and reliable today. If we will but heed him, take his advice and use it, we can build for ourselves a better America--one that both preserves his legacy and our own freedom.

NOTES:

[131] For a more detailed discussion of such a proposed amendment, see my article: Duane L. Ostler, "Legislative Oversight of a Bill of Rights: A Way to Rectify Judicial Activism," 90(5) Washington University Law Review 1581 (2013).

ABOUT THE AUTHOR

Duane L. Ostler was raised in Southern Idaho, where the wind never stops. He has lived in Australia, Mexico, Brazil, China, the big Island of Hawaii, and—most foreign of all—New Jersey. He practiced law for over a decade, then obtained a PhD in legal history. He and his wife have five children and two cats.

OTHER BOOKS BY THE AUTHOR

The Ninth Amendment: Key to Understanding the Bill of Rights

This book explains how the Ninth Amendment is the key to understanding rights in the United States. The founders created the Ninth Amendment to protect unlisted natural law rights as they were understood in their day. This amendment was never intended to allow future generations to create new rights. Rather, it was to safeguard the morality and natural rights of the founding generation.

Abortion: What the Founding Fathers Thought About It

This book gives the views of the founding fathers against abortion, and describes the surprising truth about the common law abortion rule which was misinterpreted by the court in Roe v. Wade. Most importantly, the book tells how the 9th Amendment was intended to incorporate the founders' views of natural law as part of the Constitution-which would protect the unborn from the moment of conception!

A Conversation About Abortion Between Justice Blackmun and the Founding Fathers

On a dark night in Independence Hall, ghosts of the founding fathers gather to discuss with Justice Blackmun the Roe v Wade abortion opinion he penned in 1973. Using actual quotes from the founding fathers, this debate soundly refutes Blackmun's arguments from the Roe opinion, and shows that the founders would be greatly disturbed at the law regarding abortion in America today.

How to Be Your Own Lawyer in a Non-Criminal Case in the USA (under pen name "Silas Flint")

This handy guide is written by a lawyer, and tells how to handle legal claims on your own. Topics include how to think like a lawyer, how to identify legal claims, how to conduct legal research, how to file documents at court and how to handle court appearances. The book also contains helpful information on specific legal matters such as divorce, bankruptcy, foreclosures, contract disputes, etc.

Bizarre Takings Cases in the United States and Australia (under pen name "Silas Flint")

A dispute about who owns garbage? A court case over who gets to operate San Quentin Prison? A fight regarding use of a church pew? Bizarre as these examples sound, each was a real court case in either the United States or Australia, in which the government took private property. In clear, simple language this volume presents some of the quirkier "takings" cases in legal history.

The Government Took My Property! A Comparison of Acquisition Law in Australia and the United States (under pen name "Silas Flint")

Most people don't think much about acquisitions or "takings" of private property by the government--until they receive a letter that their land is about to be taken! This complex subject is made easy to understand in this volume. The author uses zany humor and bizarre examples to describe the history of acquisitions in Australia and the USA, and how they have come to be what they are today.

<u>The First Auto Laws in the United States</u>
(under pen name "Silas Flint")

Stopping speeders by throwing logs in front of their car? Having a man walk in front of the car waving a red flag, to warn it is coming? Putting the initials of the driver on a piece of metal to act as his license plate? Giving a driver's license to anyone who has the use of both arms? These are but a few examples from this book of the first laws dealing with new-fangled automobiles.

www.ingramcontent.com/pod-product-compliance
Lightning Source LLC
Chambersburg PA
CBHW071041290526
45795CB00004B/1255